FOR
SUCH A TIME
AS THIS

FOR
SUCH A TIME
AS THIS

IAN R. K. PAISLEY

AMBASSADOR

Belfast Northern Ireland **Greenville** South Carolina

FOR SUCH A TIME AS THIS
© 1999 Ian R. K. Paisley

ISBN 1 84030 073 6

Ambassador Publications
a division of
Ambassador Productions Ltd.
Providence House
16 Hillview Avenue,
Belfast, BT5 6JR
Northern Ireland
www.ambassador-productions.com

Emerald House
1 Chick Springs Road, Suite 203
Greenville,
South Carolina 29609, USA
www.emeraldhouse.com

CONTENTS

FOREWORD
BY DR. IAN PAISLEY

This book takes a look back, takes a look forward and takes a look up.

It is geared into the new millennium. Of that it can be said as was said to all Israel when they came to cross the flooded Jordan, *"Ye have not passed this way heretofore."* Joshua 3:4.

Entering a new millennium of time is a new experience for us all. It brings new difficulties, new temptations and new trials but it also brings new challenges, new opportunities and new conquests.

What we have learned from the past will help us in the untrodden future but best of all, God who made the future will be our guide. From His throne comes the word of encouragement, *"Be not fearful but believing."*

One of the most touching words of our Lord Jesus is about the little sparrow: *"Are not two sparrows sold for a farthing? and one of them shall not fall on the ground without your heavenly Father."* Matthew 10:29.

"Are not five sparrows sold for two farthings, and not one of them is forgotten of God? But even the very hairs of your head are all numbered. Fear not therefore: ye are of more value than many sparrows." Luke 12:4,5.

His eye is on the sparrow and he watches over me.

To look back produces humility and gratitude. To look forward produces prayer and hope. To look up produces the strength for the hitherto untrodden path.

I thank all those who contributed, without them the task could not have been done.

DR. BOB JONES III , DR. KEN CONNOLLY, DR. ROD BELL, DR. BRIAN GREEN, DR. JOHN DOUGLAS, DR. ALAN CAIRNS DR. S. B. COOKE, DR. FRANK McCLELLAND, REV. JAMES BEGGS, REV. IVAN FOSTER, REV. WILLIAM BEATTIE, REV. STANLEY BARNES , REV. DAVID McILVEEN, MRS. EILEEN PAISLEY, LYDIA HUDDLESTON, SHARON HUDDLESTON, RHONDA PAISLEY, CHERITH CALDWELL , REV. KYLE PAISLEY, AND IAN PAISLEY JNR

My wife Eileen and my daughter Cherith who did all the gruelling spade work in setting and proof reading have put me even further into their debt. For them I know it has been a toil of love.

To God my Saviour, Father, Son and Holy Spirit I return my deepest thanks. Without their love and blessing there would be no such story to tell.

Ian R. K. Paisley
Belfast.
December, 1999

A TIME TO BE BORN AND A TIME TO DIE

ECCLESIASTES 3 V 2

In the third chapter of Ecclesiastes the Royal Preacher Solomon gives us a definitive statement of what "SUCH A TIME AS THIS" really is.

He describes it by what happens, what is undertaken and what is performed in that particular time.

In a series of contrasts he spells out exactly what "SUCH A TIME AS THIS" consists of.

A TIME TO BE BORN AND A TIME TO DIE
Eccles. 3:2

A time to be born and then the contrast, a time to die. (Ecclesiastes 3:2)

Solomon starts with the beginnings and contrasts the beginnings with the endings.

We need all to remind ourselves of our existence in this world, our birth, and our exit from this world, our death.

Who am I, from whence did I come? Whither am I going? These are questions we all need to ask.

A TIME TO BE BORN

David gives a divinely revealed account of our beginning. *"I will praise thee; for I am fearfully and wonderfully made; marvellous are thy works; and that my soul knoweth right well. My substance was not hid from thee, when I was made in secret, and curiously wrought in the lowest parts of the earth. Thine eyes did see my substance, yet being unperfect; and in thy book all my members were written, which in continuance were fashioned, when as yet there was none of them. How precious also are thy thoughts unto me, O God! how great is the sum of them! If I should count them, they are more in number than the sand: when I awake, I am still with thee."* Ps 139:14-18

Let us always remember, as Professor Childs Robinson so excellently put it: "We stand neither with an axiom of reason nor with a datum of experience but with what God has told us in His Word concerning Himself; His gracious invitation for our salvation and the hope He has laid up for those who trust in Him."

That leads me to the importance of the new birth contrasting with the old birth, the birth from above contrasting with the birth from beneath, the second birth contrasting with the first.

"That which is born of the flesh is flesh (that is the first birth) that which is born of the Spirit is spirit (that is the second birth). Marvel not that I said unto you, Ye must be born again ... Except a man be born again he cannot see the kingdom of God." (John 3:6-7)

The Lord Jesus pointed out to the most religious man in Jerusalem, one Nicodemus, that he must be made anew if he were ever to enter the kingdom of God.

He showed him in a well known Old Testament incident the secret of the Cross Work which He, the Saviour of the World, would perform and the way that work would be applied savingly to his sinful heart.

"And as Moses lifted up the serpent in the wilderness even so must the Son of Man be lifted up. That whosoever believeth in Him should not perish but have everlasting life." John 3:14-15.

Lifted up was He to die,
It is finished was His cry,
Now in heaven exalted high
Hallelujah! what a Saviour!

10

It is not what we can do, it is what Christ has done, which brings us into the kingdom of God. Faith is the key to the door into that kingdom.

What is faith? It is trust

F= Forsaking
A = All
I = I, (me)
T = Trust
H = Him

That is the simplicity of the gospel.

In such as time as this there are births, thousands and thousands of them. They are all human souls but "there is none born righteous no not one' Romans 3:10.

These souls, born into this fallen world of ours must hear this message of the second birth which can give to them everlasting life - life which is life indeed, life with a capital "L".

In hearing their souls can be partakers of this new birth and new life. For such a time as this it is the task of every believer to bring this message to all whom they can reach.

What Is A Minority?

We are reminded of JB Gough's immortal definition:

"What is a minority? The chosen heroes of this earth have been in a minority. There is not a social, political or religious privilege that you enjoy today that was not bought for you by the blood and tears and patient sufferings of the minority. It is the minority that has vindicated humanity in every struggle. It is a minority that has stood in the van of every moral conflict, and achieved all that is noble in the history of the world. You will find that each generation has been always busy in gathering up the scattered ashes of the martyred heroes of the past, to deposit them in the golden urn of a nation's history. Look at Scotland, where they are erecting monuments - to whom? - to the Covenanters. Ah, they were in a minority. Read their history, if you can, without the blood tingling to the tips of your fingers. These were the minority that, through blood, and tears, and beatings and scourgings - dyeing the waters with their blood and staining the heather with their gore - fought the glorious battle of religious freedom. Minority! If a man stands up for the right, though the right be on the scaffold, while the wrong sits in the seat of government; if he stand for the right, though he eat, with the right and truth, a wretched crust; if he walk with obloquy and scorn in the by-lanes and streets, while falsehood and wrong ruffle it in silken attire, let him remember that wherever the right and truth are, there are always 'Troops of beautiful tall angels' gathered round him, and God Himself stands with the dim future, and keeps watch over His own. If a man stands for the right and the truth, though every man's finger be pointed at him, though every woman's lip be curled at him in scorn, he stands in a MAJORITY, for God and good angels are with him, and greater are they that are for him than all they that be against him."

Despised and rejected, yet such a testimony will not be in vain.

A TIME TO DIE
"And a time to die"

Yes, this is another brand mark of such a time as this.

Death is all around us, physical death. Death has gained new speed.

The Black Death of the Aids virus is sweeping the continent of Africa and has laid its fangs on every country of the world. Men die in darkness at our side.

Behold the greatest of all rivers! Behold the blackness of its swift moving waters! See the multitude caught in its humanly inescapable current.

That river is death. That blackness is death. That current is death.

For we must needs die and are as water spilt on the ground which cannot be gathered up again. (We know that to be true but so is the rest of the Bible text) *Neither doth God respect any person, yet doth He devise means that His banished be not expelled from Him".* II Samuel 14:14.

Christ came just to do exactly that - He came to seek and to save that which was lost.

Physical death leads either to heaven or hell. When the souls trusting Christ alone for salvation, *"not of works lest any man should boast"* (Ephesians 2:9) die they go to be with Christ which is **far better**. Absent from the body - present with the Lord.

The soul not trusting in Christ alone is lost and goes to hell where the Lord Jesus Himself tells us "their worm dieth not and the fire is not quenched!"

Such statements of our Lord Jesus, as J H Leckie well said, "Compel us to recognise with an awe of spirit which is deeper, the more humbly we acknowledge the authority of Jesus, that He believed in an immeasurable danger which threatened the souls of men: a horror of a great darkness from which they had to be delivered."

The Lord the Judge, before His throne,
Bids the whole earth draw nigh;
The nations near the rising sun;
And near the western sky.

No more shall bold blasphemers say
Judgment will ne'er begin;
No more abuse His long delay,
To insolence and sin.

Throned on a cloud our God shall come,
Bright flames prepare His way;
Thunder and darkness, fire and storm;
Lead on the glorious day.

Heaven from above His call shall hear,
Attending angels come;
And earth and hell shall know and fear
His justice and their doom.

If the Lord Jesus Christ's return prevents it not, I too will die. My friends, and no doubt my foes, will attend my funeral. All sorts of things good, bad and indifferent will be pronounced over me and about me. When it is announced Ian Paisley is dead don't believe it. I will be living then as I have never lived before, crying, "Welcome, welcome heaven, welcome loved ones, welcome angels of God, but welcome ten million times God the Father who loved me, God the Son who died for me and God the Holy Ghost who regenerated and sanctified me - the eternal Three in One and the Eternal One in Three."

I was asked recently by the BBC's *Sunday Sequence* if I would have a clean bill of health when I came to the Pearly Gates. I simply replied:

"In peace let me resign my breath
And Thy salvation see.
My sins deserve eternal death,
But Jesus died for me."

"For to me to live is Christ and to die is gain."

On the 6th of April, 1926 I was born in Station Terrace, Armagh, Northern Ireland. I partook of the first birth which imparted death and sin to my soul.

On the 29th of May, 1932, I was born again by simple faith in our Lord Jesus Christ, in Ballymena Baptist Church, a building erected to house converts from the great '59 Revival. My mother led me to the Saviour after a children's meeting at which she spoke on John 10:11. *"I am the Good Shepherd - the Good Shepherd giveth His life for the sheep."* That day in childish simplicity I received Christ as my Saviour. Through my childhood, my teens and from my twenties to my seventies I can say I have miserably failed Christ many, many times but He has never failed me. I have been in some tight and tough places in my life but He has kept me to this day and will not let me go.

My testimony of Him is simple but very, very real. Every day with Jesus is sweeter than the day before! My prayer is, "O that my Saviour were your Saviour too!"

O death where is thy sting?
O grave where is thy victory?

The answer is non-existent to the Child of God.

"Here and now it benefits me unspeakably to look on to my last time. Here and now it is my education and sanctification and consolation to forefancy the end of ends" - Alexander Smellie.

Remember "Such a time as this" has in it a time to be born and a time to die.

Contemplation of both are essential if we are going to face the challenge of such a time as this.

A TIME TO PLANT AND A TIME TO PLUCK UP THAT WHICH IS PLANTED
ECCLESIASTES 3 V 2

The early days of our times is the time to plant. As our planting is so will be our growing be and as our growing is so will be our harvest.

I am glad that from my earliest days I was introduced to the Bible - the Authorised Version in the English language. The Old Book, as it is lovingly called - where true Protestantism still flourishes.

I would affirm with the great Prince of Preachers, C H Spurgeon, when he said: "We must defend the Faith; for what would have become of us if our fathers had not maintained it? If Confessors, Reformers, Martyrs, and Covenanters had been recreant to the name and faith of Jesus, where would have been the Churches of today? Must we not play the man as they did? If we do not, are we not censuring our Fathers? It is very pretty, is it not, to read of Luther and his brave deeds? Of course, everybody admires Luther! Yes, yes, but you do not want anyone else to do the same today. When you go to the Zoological Gardens you all admire the bear; but how would you like a bear at home, or a bear wandering loose about the street? You tell me that it would be unbearable, and no doubt you are right. So, we admire a man who is firm in the Faith, say four hundred years ago; the past ages are a sort of bear-pit or iron cage for him; but such a man today is a nuisance, and must be put down. Call him a narrow-minded bigot, or give him a worse name if you can think of one. Yet imagine that in those ages past, Luther, Zwingli, Calvin, and their compeers had said, 'The world is out of order; but if we try to set it right we shall only make a great row, and get ourselves into disgrace. Let us go to our chambers, put on our night-caps, and sleep over the bad times, and perhaps when we wake up things will have grown better.' Such conduct upon their part would have entailed upon us a heritage of error. Age after age would have gone down into the infernal deeps, and the pestiferous bogs of error would have swallowed all. These men loved the faith and the name of Jesus too well to see them trampled on. Note what we owe them, and let us pay to our sons the debt we owe to our fathers. It is today as it was in the Reformers' days, decision is needed."

A TIME TO PLANT

The first Bible I ever remember was the large Bible which my father used for the conducting of family worship in our home.

I looked on that book with special reverence. It was a book to be treasured, a book to be paid heed to, for it was the Word of God.

I learned early in simplicity what a famous divine has stated succinctly, that we can only know God by God's own self-revelation. If God had not chosen to reveal Himself in His own Word we would have no reliable information about Him - not an axiom or a datum.

That is what the Bible claims for itself and I believe it to be God's Holy Truth of God's Holy Book. The Bible's many detractors in every age pass away and are soon forgotten but the Word of the Lord endureth forever.

That big family Bible was the first book I remember reading. Its words were short in the passages chosen and easily pronounced. Its stories were gripping. It was a grand reading primer because its English is from the Saxon well, undefiled.

It lent itself to repetition. Its simple texts were easily committed to memory.

There is not a modern English version which lends itself to such vital fastening of God's truths in the minds of the young.

Little did I think that that very Bible would be destroyed by fire when Roman Catholic republican terrorists torched my parents' holiday home at Killowen, South Down and left it in ashes, having first robbed it of its furnishings.

Rome has never loved the Authorised Version of Holy Scripture. She tolerates only those versions which pander to her dogmas and add to the scriptures in order to bolster up her arrogant claims.

For "such a time as this" the Authorised Version of the Scriptures in the English tongue is the Bible we should read, honour, learn, and obey and make it as it was when it was published, the Book of the English speaking people.

He who knows not the Bible has made himself poor physically, mentally and spiritually. He has and is taking part in his own destruction.

Burns, the Bard of Scotland in *Cottars Saturday Night* describes a family altar prayer scene. Alas a scene too rare today, but universally common in Burns' day. How poverty-stricken is the home that has no such *Family Altar*.

The planting of a wholesome reverence for God's Word was the first planting in my heart. What a seed that is and what a harvest it yields.

With that planting comes the planting in the heart by the hearing of the Word of what are called the Doctrine of Grace, the great doctrines in soteriology (the doctrine of salvation). God's grace; man's sin; the way of salvation by substitutional sacrifice; redemption through Christ's blood alone; regeneration (the new birth); sanctification (being made holy) by the application of the Word of God to the heart of the sinner; and the Doctrine of the Saints Everlasting Rest.

What a planting that is! What a reaping we can expect from it. There is indeed a time to plant.

Of course there are many other spiritual doctrines and practices seeded in the Bible and by taking heed to the Bible these all will come to be planted in our hearts as well.

Where the sowing is sparingly done the harvest will be sparingly reaped.

The behaviour of a man stems from what he believes. I believe, therefore I behave the way I do. That is why faith is so important.

As the Scriptures themselves put it "As a man thinketh in his heart so is he."

Of course, there are other forces which will be sowing in such a time as this.

The Devil not only seeks to destroy the good sown seed by stealing it away. See Christ's parable of the sower in Mark 4.

He also sows tares amongst the seed as it grows, in order to destroy it.

There is a constant struggle between the two plantings, the two growings and the two harvestings.

Satan assaults those who are Christ's. He concentrates on those whom he has lost from his family, not those who are securely in his imprisoning grasp. *"But if our gospel be hid, it is hid to them that are lost: In whom the god of this world hath blinded the minds of them which believe not, lest the light of the glorious gospel of Christ, who is the image of God, should shine unto them."* (II Corinthians 4:3-4)

I remember all those plantings of the devil and all his attempts to sow his seed in my heart. The battle with Satan's sowings goes on until life ends. There is no discharge in this war.

The attempt to plant the increasing love of the pleasures of this world is Satan's ploy. How subtle, how persistent, how diligent and how deceptive are his overtures to the redeemed soul to forsake Christ and to seek satisfaction in the harlotry of his counterfeits.

For such a time as this is the time to establish in our hearts the planting of the Lord.

The apostle Paul gives a most striking testimony to the priority and permanency of the Lord's planting in his heart, in Philippians 3:4-16 *"Though I might also have confidence in the flesh. If any other man thinketh that he hath whereof he might trust in the flesh, I more: Circumcised the eighth day, of the stock of Israel, of the tribe of Benjamin, an Hebrew of the Hebrews; as touching the law, a Pharisee: Concerning zeal, persecuting the church: touching the righteousness which is in the law, blameless. But what things were gain to me, those I counted loss for Christ. Yea doubtless, and I count all things but loss for the excellency of the knowledge of Christ Jesus my Lord; for whom I have suffered the loss of all things, and do count them but dung, that I may win Christ. And be found in him, not having mine own righteousness, which is of the law, but that which is through the faith of Christ, the righteousness which is of God by faith; That I may know him, and the power of his resurrection, and the fellowship of his sufferings, being made conformable unto his death; If by any means I might attain unto the resurrection of the dead. Not as though I had already attained, either were already perfect: but I follow after, if that I may apprehend that for which also I am apprehended of Christ Jesus. Brethren, I count not myself to have apprehended: but this one thing I do, forgetting those things which are behind, and reaching forth unto those things which are before, I press toward the mark for the prize of the high calling of God in Christ Jesus. Let us therefore, as many as be perfect, be thus minded: and if in any thing ye be otherwise minded, God shall reveal even this unto you. Nevertheless, whereto we have already attained, let us walk by the same rule, let us mind the same thing."*

Here Paul sets forth:

ONE: THE CALCULATION WITHOUT ANY RE-COUNT

Paul has made his calculation. Paul has done his sums. He has got his total. That total is not for retraction or alteration. He is not going back to the drawing board. He was as fixed as the pole star to it. It is not going to be altered. It is not going to be changed. He was never going back to do his sums. For him the dye was cast eternally - as long as the sun and the moon endureth.

Note how he had carefully counted his gains. Here is his seven-fold list of those gains. These seven things were his religious motivation, his spiritual creed and his moral faith.

1. HIS OBLIGATION - *"circumcised the eighth day"* (verse 5)

He was, at eight days, made to take the sign and cutting in his flesh that he was obligating himself in life and death, he was a slave to the Covenant of Works.

He was no proselyte to the Jewish religion. He was not grafted in from a wild olive tree. He was of the true tree. Not for him as with Abram the Father of the Hebrew race, circumcision in later life. No! No! He was circumcised the eighth day, the exact time demanded by the law.

He boasted of that and of the privilege and responsibilities associated with the ritual of that act.

His circumcision was the brandmark of that God whom he served, that religion he practised, and to that faith he was totally committed. This to him was his FIRST GAIN. He was no convert. He was born a Jew.

2. HIS IDENTIFICATION - *"of the stock of Israel"*

He identified himself as being not a branch or a twig of Israel but of the stock of Israel.

He did not seek to hide his light under a bushel. He wanted everyone to know on what side he was and what his religion was. He was as open as he possibly could be.

This to him was his SECOND gain, He was no half-breed like Timothy.

3. HIS GENERATION - *"of the tribe of Benjamin"*

Benjamin was one of the most honoured tribes of Israel. It was the tribe honoured to give Israel its first king, Saul the son of Kish was a Benjamite.

The temple site was in the territory of Benjamin. This to him was his THIRD gain. He was no ordinary "five-eighth". The royal blood of Benjamin coursed in his veins.

4. HIS AFFIRMATION - *"an Hebrew of the Hebrews"*

What a Jesuit is in the Church of Rome so Paul was in Jewry. He was the creme-de-la-creme. He was no counterfeit coin. This to him was his FOURTH gain.

5. HIS CLASSIFICATION - *"as touching the law, a Pharisee"*

He was of the strictest sect of the Jews, a Pharisee. He was a fundamentalist of Jewish fundamentalists as far as the Jewish law was concerned.

This to him was his FIFTH gain. He was no heretic.

6. HIS DEDICATION - *"concerning zeal, persecuting the church"*

He was no follower of another religion. He hated dissent. He loathed those who didn't bow to Jewry. This was his SIXTH gain. He was no schismatic.

7. HIS ESTIMATION - *"as touching the righteousness which is in the law, blameless"*

Paul carried out every commandment of righteousness in the law of the Jews.

He was a legalist, a slave to the tradition of the elders.

This to him was his SEVENTH gain.

He was no rebel. He was morally exact in his own eyes, though totally immoral in the eyes of a Thrice Holy God.

Firstly, Paul counted these seven gains - verse 7.

Secondly, Paul counted these as loss for Christ - verse 7.

Thirdly, Paul counted all these but loss - verse 8.

Fourthly, Paul counted them but "dung".

He repudiated them in the day of his conversion, but after twenty-five years he reprobated them. They are but dung (the offal cast to dogs).

The first repudiation is important but the final reprobation is much more important. After a quarter of a century the apostle maintained his original consistency.

TWO: THE CONCLUSION WITHOUT ANY CHANGE

"Yea doubtless" Phil. 3:8

Paul did not rethink his position. He came once and for all to an unshakable conclusion. He is grounded on unchangeable granite. His position is not up for argument, discussion or debate. It is final. It is settled.

It is forever an eternal in time.

Paul's mind is sealed. He stands and is determined to remain standing. He is handcuffed, shackled, bound and imprisoned to this conviction and conclusion.

His every doubt has been laid to rest.

His vision of the Saviour on the Damascus Road was final. It locked out and buried forever all former convictions. All his doubts were buried and he had been brought into the liberty of the sons of God. *"Ye shall know the truth,"* the Lord Jesus had said, *"and the truth shall make you free"* (John 8:32). Paul was liberated from the slavery of Satan and sin forever, and had become now and for all time and eternity the bondslave of Christ.

THREE: THE CHRIST WITHOUT ANY COMPETITION

"Yea doubtless, and I count all things but loss for the excellency of the knowledge of Christ Jesus my Lord: for whom I have suffered the loss of all things, and do count them but dung, that I may win Christ." Phil. 3:8

Paul talks about *"winning Christ"*.

Paul talks about *"the excellency of the knowledge of Christ Jesus my Lord"*

He testifies that he has lost all things for Him, yet he knows no loss. He states rather that he is infinitely the gainer.

The excellency of this knowledge is in its finding - *"to be found in Christ"*. The excellency of this knowledge is in its righteousness - *"not having my own righteousness which is of the law"*.

His religion is not a number of theological axioms but a living, loving, personal Saviour,

Whose Resurrection is Power;

Whose Suffering is Fellowship;

Whose Death is Conformity.

O Christ He is the fountian,
The deep sweet well of love.
The streams on earth I've tasted,
More deep I'll drink above -
There, to an ocean fullness,
His mercy doth expand,
And glory, deathless, dwelleth
In Emmanuel's land.

FOUR: THE COMMITMENT WITHOUT ANY COMPROMISE

"Not as though I had already attended, either were already perfect: but I follow after, if that I may apprehend that for which also I am apprehended of Christ Jesus" Phil. 3:12

Paul had been apprehended by Christ. He had been arrested. He had never been released from that arrest. In fact he wanted above all things, to reciprocate, to arrest Christ, to apprehend Christ, to captivate Christ.

"*That I might apprehend*". Here was a commitment which would not know or want to know any compromise. "Christ's forever, only His."

This is the unbreakable bond. This is the eternal vision.

This is the blessed Oneness.

This is the life of the Lord Jesus lived out in us "*I am crucified with Christ: nevertheless I live; yet not I, but Christ liveth in me: and the life which I now live in the flesh I live by the faith of the Son of God, who loved me, and gave himself for me.*" Galatians 2:20.

This is God beseeching sinners by us, "*Now then we are ambassadors for Christ, as though God did beseech you by us: we pray you in Christ's stead, be ye reconciled to God.*" II Corinthians 5:20.

FIVE: THE CONTENDING WITHOUT ANY CONTRACTING

"*Brethren, I count not myself to have apprehended: but this one thing I do, forgetting those things which are behind, and reaching forth unto those things which are before. I press toward the mark for the prize of the high calling of God in Christ Jesus.*" Phil. 3:13,14.

Here is a contending without any contracting.

Here is a running without any slacking.

Here is a sprinting without any tiring.

Here is a stickability without any let-up.

The motivation for such contending was:

1. Forgetfulness - "*forgetting those things that are behind*".
2. Forwardness - "*reaching forth unto those things which are before*".
3. Faithfulness - "*I press*"
4. Fullness - "*This one thing I do*".

"No turning back," cried the apostle, as he ran as one who would obtain (I Corinthians 9:24).

So let us all run in such a time as this, so that we also shall obtain.

This shall be our portion as we know the Lord's planting.

A TIME TO PLUCK UP THAT WHICH IS PLANTED

Now we come to the opposite of planting. Yes, in such a time as this there is time for planting (Ecclesiastes 3:2) but in such a time as this there is also a time for plucking up that which is planted.

There is not only a rooting but an uprooting. The Blessed Master taught us that *"Every plant, which my heavenly Father hath not planted, shall be rooted up."* (Matthew 15:13).

There is a constructive ministry but also a destructive ministry. The gospel is a savour of life unto life or of death unto death (Jeremiah 21:8).

The occupations and demonstrations of life in such a time as this are great in number, manifold in variety, contradictory in their relations, and bounded in their durations.

There is a time! There is a time!! There is a time!!!

There is such a time as this~ - as this!! as this!!!

But there are common factors in our life lived out in the time appointed to us.

The purposes of our life are divinely ordered.

The periods of our life are divinely ordered.

The providences of our life are divinely ordered.

The programmes of our life are divinely ordered.

The perils of our life are divinely ordered.

Our times have mysteries to contemplate, beauties to admire, work to accomplish, good to participate in, and plans to fulfil.

There is a time to pluck up that which is planted just as there is a time to plant.

There are growings that must be cut down, buildings which must be levelled, forests which must be cleared and weeds which must be eradicated.

Remember God's word to Jeremiah *"See, I have this day set thee over the nations and over the kingdoms, to root out, and to pull down, and to destroy and to throw down, to build, and to plant."* Jeremiah 1:10. Here was a fourfold destructive ministry.

1. *A rooting out* - the utter destruction of the very roots - the undergrowth. There is a time to pluck out.

2. *A pulling down* - no matter how high the building, down it must come - a time to pluck up.

3. *A destroying* - no matter how pleasing the edifice, it must be devastated - a time to pluck up.

4. *A throwing down* - no matter how pleasing the growth, it must be thrown down by force - a time to pluck up.

There is also a two fold constructive ministry.

1. To build.
2. To plant.

They are closely associated in such a time as this.

Our Lord's ministry commenced with a destructive act. He commenced His ministry by cleansing the Temple *"And the Jews' passover was at hand, and Jesus went up to Jerusalem, And found in the temple those that sold oxen and sheep and doves, and the changers of money sitting: And when he had made a scourge of small cords, he drove them all out of the temple, and the sheep and the oxen; and poured out the changers' money, and overthrew the tables; And said unto them that sold doves, Take these things hence; make not my Father's house an house of merchandise. And his disciples remembered that it was written, The zeal of thine house hath eaten me up"* John 2:13-17.

He concluded His ministry by cleansing the Temple the second time *"And Jesus went into the temple of God, and cast out all them that sold and bought in the temple, and overthrew the tables of the moneychangers, and the seats of them that sold doves. And said unto them, It is written, My house shall be called the house of prayer; but ye have made it a den of thieves."* Matthew 21: 12-13, *"And they come to Jerusalem: and Jesus went into the temple, and began to cast out them that sold and bought in the temple, and overthrew the tables of the moneychangers, and the seats of them that sold doves; And would not suffer that any man should carry any vessel through the temple."* Mark 11:15-16 *"And he went into the temple, and began to cast out them that sold therein, and them that bought; Saying unto them, It is written, My house is the house of prayer: but ye have made it a den of thieves."* Luke 19:45-46.

The consistent ministry of Christ was not only constructive of good but destructive of evil. There was no change in that. He commenced, continued and concluded in that manner.

He plucked down the planting that was not of His Father. He preserved the planting that was of His Father.

Through good report or ill report we must pluck down all evil. This is our task. We must follow faithfully the example and commandments of our Master.

Such a time as this is a time of plucking down that which is planted by the Satanic sower of tares.

To do such a plucking down men cry, "It will leave us in a small minority." What of that! God's minorities are always victorious. If God be for us who can be against us?

It was the challenge of these truths which brought me in 1951 to make the momentous decision that the time had come to declare without fear or favour the biblical doctrine of separation from the great apostasy and to call the people of God out from the entanglements of ecclesiastical compromise and the uncleanness of the ecumencial movement. This was the message then *"for such a time as this"* and it is the same message for the millennium to come.

Separated churches across the world stand witness to the faithfulness of God and the power of His eternal truth.

A group of people who owned no property but believed God's Word, proved in a marvellous way what God could do for those sold out on His Word. Today the value of those properties alone, many millions and millions, is a standing testimony to the prosperity which comes when God's people are outside the camp to bear reproach for the sake of our Lord Jesus Christ. Outside the camp is surely within the veil *"And Moses took the tabernacle, and pitched it without the camp, afar off from the camp, and called it the Tabernacle of the congregation. And it came to pass, that every one which sought the Lord went out unto the tabernacle of the congregation, which was without the camp. And it came to pass, when Moses went out unto the tabernacle, that all the people rose up, and stood every man at his tent door, and looked after Moses, until he was gone into the tabernacle. And it came to pass, as Moses entered into the tabernacle, the cloudy pillar descended, and stood at the door of the tabernacle, and the Lord talked with Moses. And all the people saw the cloudy pillar stand at the tabernacle door: and all the people rose up and worshipped, every man in his tent door. And the Lord spake unto Moses face to face, as a man speaketh unto his friend. And he turned again into the camp: but his servant Joshua, the son of Nun, a young man, departed not out of the tabernacle."* Exodus 33:7-11.

Oh to be a Joshua and remain within the veil!

Jesus, I my cross have taken,
All to leave and follow Thee;
Destitute, despised, forsaken,
Thou from hence my all shalt be.

I will follow Thee, my Saviour,
Thou didst shed Thy blood for me,
And though all the world forsake me,
By Thy grace I'll follow Thee.

Perish ev'ry fond ambition,
All I've sought, and hoped, and known;
Yet how right is my condition!
God and heaven are still mine own.

Let the world despise and leave me:
They have left my Saviour too -
Human hearts and looks deceive me -
Thou art not, like them, untrue.

And whilst Thou shalt smile upon me,
God of wisdom, love and might,
Foes may hate, and friends disown me;
Show Thy face and all is bright.

Man may trouble and distress me,
'Twill but drive me to Thy breast;
Life with trials hard may press me,
Heaven will bring me sweeter rest.

Oh! 'tis not in grief to harm me,
While Thy love is left to me;
Oh! 'twere not in joy to charm me,
Were that joy unmixed with Thee.

T. Myron Webb calls the number of the Moderinst: "Modernism is the Devil's most effective weapon. With it he severs every restraining cable from the tower of faith. With its black mantle he dims every spiritual light. Modernism is a wild Absalom of rebellion. It is a cruel Ahab of 'selling out to wickedness'. It is a treacherous Jezebel of Pagan worship. It is a 'Simon the Sorcerer' or merchandising the ministry for gain. It is a scoffing 'Sanballat and Tobiah', mocking and scoffing at all constructive building for God. In comparison to Modernism, all pagan philosophies sink into insignificance. The

Modernist wears the breast-plate of Christianity to hide a hide burned black by the fires of hell. The Modernist parades behind the innocent mask of a lamb which hides the snarl of the wolf. He parades under the banner of enlightenment but walks in the darkness of the damned. He professes to be an exponent of liberty but in reality is in the bondage of corruption. The children of God are not ignorant of Satan's devices. But the unsaved world is bound and gagged, fettered and chained, by the Modernist preacher, who is the agent and representative of the power of darkness."

"*Let us go forth therefore unto Him* (our Lord Jesus Christ) *without* [outside] *the Camp, bearing His reproach.*" (Heb 13:13).

"This is the day! This is the hour!
To prove our God's almighty power;
To follow Him whate'er befall,
And answer gladly to His call -
To go 'Without the Camp!'

Apart from those who doubt His Word,
From those who have denied your Lord!
Oh, Christian, hasten to His side,
Who for your sin was crucified -
And go 'Without the Camp!'

'Tis only now that we can bear
In His reproach, our little share.
He did not stop to count the cost
When going forth to save the lost -
He went 'Without the Camp!'

And though you here may stand alone, -
At that Great Day, upon His Throne,
In robes of righteousness arrayed -
What joy to know the choice you made -
To go 'Without the Camp!'"

For such a time as this - a time to pluck up that which is planted.

In our first two pairs of timing the best comes first - *"a time to be born"* and *"a time to plant"* and the worst second - *"a time to die"* and *"a time to pluck up that which is planted"*.

Then the order is reversed for the next ten pairs. The worst comes first - *"a time to weep"*, and the best second - *"a time to laugh"* and so until the last of these ten pairs - *"a time to keep silent"* and *"a time to speak"*.

Then the order changes again in verse 8, the best comes first - *"a time to love"* and the worst last - *"a time to hate"*, ending with the reverse order, the worst comes first again - *"a time of war"*, and the best comes last again - *"a time of peace"*.

A TIME TO KILL AND A TIME TO HEAL
ECCLESIASTES 3 V 3

A TIME TO KILL

A time to kill for such a time as this.

No doubt this reference is to judicial killing. Capital punishment is the law of God. For capital crimes there is divinely appointed capital punishment.

"For such a time as this" criminals who have taken away the life of others must suffer the penalty of their deeds.

The British Government says "Not so" and so the most blood-thirsty murderers, guilty of multiple murders do not die but instead are released on the streets, free to engage in more such murders. They are still permitted to murder and keep their weapons.

That same Government gives legal support to the murder of the innocents.

What are the facts?

From 1968-1990 three and a half million abortions took place in England, Wales and Scotland. Since 1990 approximately 500,000 take place every year in the United Kingdom. An increase in teenage pregnancies means an increasing number of abortions are administered on teenage girls. Almost one quarter of all abortions are administered on girls below the age of 19. Thirty-two percent are administered on women between 20-24.

"For such a time as this," judicial killing is the law of God, and in its violation there is a dreadful reaping when the Thrice Holy God makes acquisition for the blood of the innocent. God will enforce a terrible payment on the wrong-doers.

Always note that out of its own time - a time to kill - killing becomes murder (See I Kings 2 and Jeremiah 12:3).

Those who oppose the punishment of the murderer and practise, support, and advocate child murders in the womb, also stand forth and scorn, deny and deride the eternal punishment of the lost in Hell.

That eternal truth was fully revealed to us by the Son of God's Love when He came to seek and to save the lost souls of sinful men and women.

If the Gentle Jesus, the Lover of the guilty souls of men and women, spoke so solemnly on this matter, should we not pay instant heed?

Denying unpalatable truth does not alter it or destroy it.

The divine law is inflexible. *"The soul that sinneth it shall die."*

Yes, die it must and die it shall. Sin is a killer.

This text is a warning about our own mortality. We too shall be killed off. *"Yea, for thy sake are we killed all the day long; we are counted as sheep for the slaughter."* Psalm 44:22. *"As it is written, For thy sake we are killed all the day long; we are accounted as sheep for the slaughter."* Romans 8:36.

We do not live here forever. We are born with our faces towards "sundown". The place which knows us today will know us no more forever. The sands of time are fast running out for us all. It behoves us to number (to count, to add up) our days that we may apply ourselves unto saving wisdom.

"For such a time as this" - there is a time to kill.

The disease which is going to kill off our body may well be at work already.

Readiness to die is the necessary requirement, and it can not be supplied by church or religion, but only by the Blood and Righteousness of the Only Saviour of the sinner, Jesus Christ our Lord.

A TIME TO HEAL

Jerusalem was in a dreadful state. The mighty King of Assyria had sworn to destroy it. It seemed it would follow in the death train of the capitals of other countries which had been devastated by the same vile dictator.

But *"in such a time as this"* it was time for healing. Mark God's judgment on the wicked king. For Zedekiah there was a time to kill but also a time to heal (see Jeremiah 34:2-5).

God's greatest healing times have been in the midst of terrible killing times. We think of the early persecution of the saints, the Reformation, the Revolution of 1688-1690 and the events in our Province since its inception.

When the enemy was certain of victory, God turned the tables, and from the jaws of death marched forth a triumphant living victorious church.

Christ does build His church and the gates of hell cannot prevail against it.

How much the Free Presbyterian Church has proved this.

Since its inception every effort has been made to destroy its leaders and its people.

Terence O'Neill announced its demise and the demise of myself. He is forgotten (I took his seat in Parliament) but the Free Presbyterian Church marches on, proclaiming without compromise the full gospel of Jesus Christ.

The contendings and confession of the church were ridiculed and mocked but God turned the enemies' mocking to their own confusion.

When John Wylie, Ivan Foster and I were imprisoned in 1966 our enemies thought they had written the obituary notice of the Free Presbyterian Church of Ulster. They planned it for evil but God meant it for good. I remember after we had done our time in jail we toured the Province and our text was Philippians 1:12-14 *"But I would ye should understand, brethren, that the things which happened unto me have fallen out rather unto the furtherance of the gospel; So that my bonds in Christ are manifest in all the palace, and in all other places; And many of the brethren in the Lord, waxing confident by my bonds, are much more bold to speak the word without fear."*

Yes, the gospel was furthered. Scores and scores of souls were soundly converted. In my own congregation, I gave the right hand of fellowship to two hundred new members. It was the dawning of the time to heal. Many new churches were formed at the time, which we called the Prison Churches.

What demonstrations of spiritual power!

What manifestation of saving grace!

What interventions of supernatural providences!

What permanent fruit in the most inclement weathers!

Our God does all things well!

We know that in eternity with the rugged but charming Covenanter Samuel Rutherford,

"We'll bless the hand that guided,
We'll bless the heart that planned,
When throned where Glory dwelleth
In Emmanuel's Land."

But now here below, with Isaac Watts we can join and sing,

The men of grace have found,
Glory begun below;
Celestial fruits on earthly ground
From faith and hope may grow.

The hill of Zion yields
A thousand sacred sweets,
Before we reach the heavenly fields
Or walk the golden streets.

How we tasted with delight those sweets, and basked in the glory we had seen in the face of Our Beloved - the glory of God in the face of Jesus Christ.

There is no presence like the presence of the Lord.

There is no joy like the joy of Jesus Christ.

There is no happiness like the happiness of the Happy God. *"The gospel of the Blessed God."* I Timothy 1:11. *'Blessed'* means *'Happy'*.

Oh that the rich streams of God's healing waters might flow forth in mighty torrents all over our Province. In those days one of the favourite hymns sung with great gusto by our congregations was:

I've cast my heavy burdens down
on Canaan's happy shore,
I'm living where the healing waters flow;
I'll wander in the wilderness of
doubt and sin no more
I'm living where the healing waters flow.

Living on the shore, I'm living on the shore,
I'm living where the healing waters flow.

With Israel's trusting children I'm
rejoicing on my way,
I'm living where the healing waters flow;
The cloudy, fiery pillar is my
guiding light today,
I'm living where the healing waters flow.

My hungering soul is satisfied with
manna from above,
I'm living where the healing waters flow.
No more I thirst, the Rock I've found,
that fount of endelss love,
I'm living where the healing waters flow.

I'm singing 'Hallelujah,' safely anchored
is my soul,
I'm living where the healing waters flow;
I'm resting on His promises, the
blood has made me whole,
I'm living where the healing waters flow.

Days of deep trial? Yes!
Days of misrepresentation? Yes!
Days of overwhelming trials? Yes!

Times of difficulties become seasons of zealous endeavour; times of darkness become days of eager anticipation of the dawning of a new day; periods of affliction become lessons of discipline in the school of experience and disappointments become the birthplace of hope in our pilgrimage to heaven.

It was in those days that lasting friendships were forged, never to be broken but by the stroke of death, friendships by the grace of God we will renew in eternal strength in our Father's House of many mansions.

The experience of a healed people is, as the Scotsman put it, "is better felt than telt".

It is a spiritual reality when deep calleth unto deep in the human soul and God's happy land is not far far away but right inside us. The Master, our blessed Jesus, was right when He said, "the kingdom of heaven is within you."

"Behold, I stand at the door, and knock: if any man hear my voice, and open the door, I will come in to him, and will sup with him, and he with me. To him that overcometh will I grant to sit with me in my throne, even as I also overcame, and am set down with my Father in his throne." Revelation 3:20-21.

For such a time as this - Supper time indeed! A time to heal.

A TIME TO BREAK DOWN AND A TIME TO BUILD UP
ECCLESIASTES 3 V 3

A TIME TO BREAK DOWN

This brings us on to the building site. The end, the objective, is to build up - a time to build up. That however is preceded by *a time to break down*. There can be no building progress until we go for a proper demolition on the site. Clearing the site is the first and onerous task. It must be done deliberately, decisively and effectually.

Solomon had this pre-building operation on a massive scale to accomplish before he laid one great stone in place on the temple site.

Nehemiah was much hindered in his re-building programme because the breaking down work was not accomplished. Much rubbish blockaded his progress.

There must be the clearing of the site. Foundation work is of first importance. Today the site of the Church's activities is blocked with the ruins of past errors or the gerry building of new innovations of this so-called super intelligent 20th century.

In 1951 the vision that my brethren and myself had was that we must make clearance for the building of God's house. The site must be cleared. All material of the devil and that of his servants of his creed, and of his synagogue, must be broken down and removed. God's Holy Book must be our only infallible rule of faith and practice. *"To the law and to the testimony: if they speak not according to this word, it is because there is no light in them"* Isaiah 8:2.

The rushlight of infidelity and blatant unbelief must be expelled by the Light of Holy Scripture.

A glory gilds the sacred page,
Majestic like the sun.
It gives a light to every age,
It gives but borrows none.

The candle of Romish superstition and the flickering match of rationalism must be removed. The Light of the Bible which alone can illuminate the path from the City of Destruction, via the Cross, to the City of God, must shine from the pulpit.

Away with the baubles of Babylon! Away with the darkness of man's polluted and perverted mind! We want the sunshine of the Redeemer's love to shine, and the light of His glorious gospel to radiate.

C H Spurgeon, the unchallengable Prince of English preachers, was right when he said, *"The Word of God is quite sufficient to interest and bless the souls of men throughout all time and all novelties soon fall."*

Apostate Protestantism, having repudiated the Infallible Bible, shaken off the gospel as a viper, utilised ecumenism as the dearest religious creed, and finally will put on black popery as a comfortable shroud in which to die.

It was no new ensign the Free Presbyterian Church unfurled on St. Patrick's Day, 17th March, 1951.

With grand old John Knox we could proclaim, *"It is not a new and strange ensign which I have unfurled but Thy noble standard, O Lord."*

With Archibald Johnson of Warrington we could cry that founding day, *"Christ lives and reigns alone in His Church and will have all done therein according to His Word and Will. He has given no Headship over His church to any Pope, King or Parliament."*

We had learned the wisdom of John Welsh who stated, *"All the compromises which have ever been made in the cause of God have always strengthened the enemy, done injury to the truth, enfeebled the weak and were never to this day joined with a blessing."*

So we had to break down the barriers which kept the gospel from being preached in all its fullness.

There must be no bluntin of the sharp points of truth or covering over with pulpit velvet the sharp threshing teeth of God's Everlasting Gospel.

The Truth, the naked truth must be proclaimed. No dressing up and doing a cosmetic job on the Old Evangel.

It must be proclaimed, in such a time as this, in all its plainness. It requires no doctoring - not in the words which man's wisdom teacheth but in the power and demonstration of the Holy Ghost. Clear a way for its deliverance!

Its power is not imparted by the preacher, he rather is empowered by its unction. Only when the preacher is mastered by the gospel can he himself master the art of proclaiming it.

George W Ridout said it well *"We are suffering today from a weak pulpit and pointless preaching. We have clever speakers but few prophets; we have too few fearless speakers for God and the truth. We have the best paid and best educated ministry but too much of it is popular, flabby and insipid and stirs neither heaven nor hell. We sadly lack men to whom the pulpit is a throne of power; we have too many flying kites of superficial thinking instead of men of fire whose utterances burn and whose sermons scorch the wicked. We have too many who coddle the saints and fail to collar the sinner."*

The Kirk Session of Lissara Presbyterian Church, Crossgar, Co. Down, Northern Ireland wanted the Gospel preached. The Presbytery of Down didn't, hence the closing of the doors against the Gospel of Christ.

The issue had to be faced. The dye had to be cast. The stand had to be taken. The banner had to be unfurled. So it was.

The press reports of that day were interesting.

Think of the scene. In Crossgar, a small village in County Down, Northern Ireland, in a small tin church once used by the Methodists for extension work in Belfast, a group of people met after an evangelistic mission when some 94 souls publicly professed faith in Jesus Christ (whole families being saved), on St Patrick's Day, 17th March, 1951.

They met to unfurl the Banner of the Lord's Truth and declare war on religious apostasy in the Irish Presbyterian Church. A young man of 24 years of age who had been the preacher in the campaign was the preacher and leader.

March 12th - Belfast Telegraph Report

"A new congregation - Crossgar congregation of the Free Presbyterian Church of Ulster is to be constituted in the Killyleagh Street Mission Hall, Crossgar, on Saturday.

This split in Presbyterians in Crossgar has resulted from a recent refusal of Down Presbytery to sanction the use of Lissara Presbyterian Church lecture hall for an evangelical mission and because the church polling list was revised, according to some of the members, contrary to the rules of the Presbyterian Church. This development was disclosed in Belfast today by Mr George K Gibson ARIBA, one of the two elders of Lissara who officially protested against the mission ruling.

He said the new congregation would have five of the seven elders of Lissara, including the Clerk of Session, Mr James Morrison, who would become the Clerk of the new Session.

Mr Gibson stated that interest in the Crossgar move had been manifested in various parts of Northern Ireland, and that some other congregations of the Free Church of Ulster were in process of formation.

Among those elders who are joining the new church are Mr W Miscampbell, superintendent of the Lissara Sabbath School; Mr Hugh James Adams, a Sabbath School teacher; and Mr C Harvey, captain of the Boys' Brigade Company. All the Sabbath School teachers are leaving to join the new congregation.

Minister, pro tem, will be Rev George Stears, of the Presbyterian Church of Brazil. He was for 22 years in the mission field there and has been resident in Belfast temporarily for the past few years.

Mr Stears expects to carry on with his missionary work but has agreed to take over the pulpit of the Crossgar congregation pending the appointment of a permanent minister.

Reason For Breakaway

This morning a letter, authorised by the five elders, was delivered by post to every member of Lissara Presbyterian Church, and to all ministers in Down Presbytery, setting out the reasons for the breakaway.

After referring to Presbytery's refusal to allow the church hall to be used for a mission, the letter deals with an alleged violation of the Presbyterian Code by the revision of the congregation polling list while the pulpit was vacant.

It states that the revision was carried out although it had been stated publicly that that could not be done, and adds:

"It is significant that our Clerk of Session, Mr James Morrison, refused to sign the revised poll list against his conscience, and others of the Session also refused even to attend the meeting at which it was confirmed."

Answer To Problem

The letter states that the answer to the problem confronting Irish Presbyterianism today was to be found in the Assembly's College, where some of the professors "both in their teachings and writings deny the truths we hold so dear, reduce the Scriptures to the level of mere human writing, make little of our Confession of Faith and Shorter Catechism, deny the very Deity and Virgin birth of our Saviour, and place the Protestant doctrine that Christ bore our sins on the Cross on a level with the Roman Catholic doctrine of the Mass."

The constitutional service at Crossgar on Saturday will be followed by the ordination and induction of the elders and the induction of Mr Stears. The service will be conducted by Rev Ian R K Paisley, of Ravenhill Evangelical Church, Belfast."

St. Patrick's Day, March 17th, 1951
Constitution And Formation Of The Crossgar Congregation
Northern Whig Report

Scenes reminiscent of an old-time revival meeting marked the formal constitution in Crossgar on Saturday afternoon of the first congregation of the "Free Presbyterian Church of Ulster."

Bus loads of evangelical Presbyterians from distant parts of Ulster turned up to swell the throng which overflowed from the little Killyleagh Street mission hall which, in the first weeks since the schism started in the congregation of Lissara Presbyterian Church, has been transformed into a temporary church building, even to a stained glass window bearing the emblem of the new denomination - burning bush and the motto - "Christ for Ulster".

A large number of Presbyterians, led by five of the original seven elders of the Lissara Church, have formed the new congregation in a general protest against "modernism" in the Irish Presbyterian Church, and in particular against the action of Down Presbytery in refusing to permit the holding of an "old-time gospel campaign" in Lissara Church hall.

Killyleagh Street hall was too small to hold all the supporters of the "breakaway" movement on Saturday, and many latecomers sat on forms outside, listening to the service through loud-speakers.

The Rev Ian RK Paisley, minister of Ravenhill Evangelical Church, Belfast, conducted the service constituting the new church and inducting the ruling elders and the temporary minister, The Rev George Stears, of the Presbyterian church of Brazil.

Solemnity, Enthusiasm

Quiet solemnity marked the actual ceremonial, but

earlier, as Mr Paisley told the reasons for the break-away - "We are going back to the old standards to preach the old Gospel" - and accused the Irish Presbyterian Church of having "betrayed the faith of our fathers," he was constantly interrupted by cries of "Hallelujah", "Amen" and "Praise the Lord".

This enthusiasm reached its highest pitch as Mr Paisley ended his sermon with the words: "Just as the Free Church of Scotland grew in strength till it was almost as big as the church it left, so I believe that this Church with the blessing of God, will go forward till all Ulster rings with its teaching."

Mr George K Gibson and Mr Hugh J Adams, two former Lissara elders who were suspended by Down Presbytery when they protested against the banning of the gospel, were inducted as elders of the new church, others being Messrs James Morrison, William Miscampbell, William Emerson and Cecil Harvey.

Belfast News Letter report - Church Constituted At Crossgar General Assembly Accused of "Modernism"

Every seat was taken in the Killyleagh Street Church Hall, Crossgar, on Saturday afternoon, when the Rev Ian RK Paisley, of Ravenhill Evangelical Church, Belfast, conducted the opening service constituting the Crossgar congregation of the Free Presbyterian Church of Ulster. Extra forms had to be brought in to accommodate the congregation. There were two special bus loads of people from Belfast and visitors from centres in Down, Antrim, Londonderry and Tyrone. The service was relayed by loud-speakers to the street.

Minister Pro Tem

The Rev George Stears, of the Presbyterian Church of Brazil, who, Mr Paisley said, was ordained to the ministry at a Presbytery meeting in Rio Grande del Norte, Brazil in May, 1935, was inducted as minister pro tem by Mr Paisley. Five elders of Lissara Presby-terian Church, from which the seceding church is a breakaway, were inducted as elders of the congre-gation. They are Messrs James Morrison (clerk), William Miscampbell, Hugh J Adams, Cecil Harvey and George K Gibson. Mr William Emerson was ordained and installed as an elder.

Mr Paisley, in the course of his sermon, said that they took their stand that day for the infallibility of the Word of God. They believed that the Bible from Genesis to Revelation was God's inspired, infallible revelation. When modernists were forgotten and heretics were no more the Word of God would stand for ever.

"We are not Unitarians," he declared. "We have no truck with Unitarians, whether they call themselves non-subscribers or whether they take the false title of First Presbyterians. WE are Trinitarians."

He would debate with any leader of the Irish Presbyterian Church in any hall in Belfast his statement that the Irish Presbyterian Church, in its General Assembly, had betrayed her position as an evangelical Protestant Church, and had allowed modernism and rationalism to take the seat of authority and rule her with ecclesiastical dictatorship.

The "lengthy epistle" which had been issued by Down Presbytery would be answered point by point. It was not true to say that it was the friends of the new congregation who wanted the Lissara poll list revised. They had protested that at an election held in Lissara Church there were people who had voted illegally. They took it to Down Presbytery who had no option but to cancel the election, but cancelling an election did not mean cancelling the poll list.

Mr Paisley said that people in Crossgar had asked themselves what was wrong with Irish Presbyterian-ism, when it did not want the Gospel in its church hall and when it suspended elders who stood up for the rights of the people.

Referring to Mr Stears, he said that Church House knew very well who he was, and Down Presbytery could have found out from Church House who he was. As for himself, he (Mr Paisley) had never claimed to be a minister of the Irish Presbyterian Church. He did not want to be associated with a church which challenged the Word of God. He was the minister of a church at Ravenhill which 14 years ago had done the same thing that Crossgar was doing today, and which had then been given by its enemies a year to last. Today it was flourishing.

"They say you cannot form a congregation because the Code forbids it," said Mr Paisley. "We have no truck with the Code. Irish Presbyterianism has sold the pass. It has betrayed the heritage of our fathers. We in Crossgar are going back to the old standards and to preach the faith of our fathers.

"Just as the Free Church of Scotland grew in strength, so we believe that this Church will have the blessing of God and go forward until Ulster rings with its teachings."

Morning and evening services were held in Killyleagh Street Hall which is a temporary worshipping place for the congregation, yesterday, and a Sunday School was held in the morning.

The background to the secession was one of heart-searching and prayer for guidance. Some facts about this can be given.

The Free Presbyterian Church of Ulster

The dictatorial, anti-evangelical and anti-evangelistic attitude of the Presbytery of Down caused much heart searching amongst the Evangelical members of the congregation. As the mission continued, conferences were held and prolonged seasons of prayer engaged in and the face of God earnestly sought for grace and wisdom to know and to do His will. The banning of the gospel and the violation of church law and the feeble explanation of Rev Bailie in regard to his actions, revealed further the depths to which the Presbytery were prepared to go in order to thwart the wishes of the majority of Evangelicals in Lissara.

Owing to the fact that certain brethren within the Irish Presbyterian Church both ministerial and lay, refused to yield full obedience to the commands of the Lord and even disregarded solemn promises made to their brethren, we feel that for the present, so that we may not be accused of jeopardising their position in the apostasy to which they still tenaciously cling, their names should go unmentioned.

Those of us who have paid the price and jeopardised all for the cause and rejoice in being counted worthy so to do, do not want any reluctant and compromising brother to suffer at the hands of the apostasy for actions with which at the time he agreed, but which he found he could not implement because of the price.

Perhaps at some distant future when personalities are forgotten, the revealing story will be told of those who started out but found the pathway too difficult and hard. In mercy, we will keep the curtain drawn over the misguided and compromising brethren. May God in His grace lead them back to the paths of obedience. At present, like Samson, their locks are shorn.

Day of Prayer and Fasting

A special day of prayer and fasting was held in Ravenhill at the conclusion of which the way of God was plain as day, and the brethren knew that God had called them to tread where the saints had trod outside the camp and then by the way of the cross, to the uplands of God.

Each individual fought a personal battle, but the victory was a united one, and each brother rejoiced together. That day of days the Free Presbyterian Church was born and brought forth in tears, agony and passion

There was such a time as this, a time for breaking down.

A TIME TO BUILD UP

To build a separated Presbyterian witness anywhere is a difficult task but to build it in Ulster is the most difficult of all.

Besides the large Irish Presbyterian Church, the largest Protestant Church in Ulster, there are three smaller bodies taking the name of Presbyterian. There is the Reformed Presbyterian Church, the Covenanters. There is the Evangelical Presbyterian Church and there is the Non-Subscribing Presbyterian Church which is Unitarian in its doctrine as is seen in its church catechism.

The Free Presbyterian Church is not only the largest of these three smaller denominations but is larger than the three all put together. So what I said at the beginning in Crossgar has become true indeed, and all Ulster has rung with its message. "Christ and Him Crucified". God has been pleased to honour the stand. To His Name be all the glory!

For such a time as this there is a time to build, and build we have and build we must.

The Free Presbyterian Church marked the way forward in its manifesto.

FREE PRESBYTERIAN MANIFESTO

Dear Friend and Member of Lissara Congregation,

Knowing that you have a keen interest in our glorious Presbyterian and Protestant heritage we address to you the following appeal.

Our Presbyterian forefathers, zealous for the Truth of God as contained in the sacred pages of our Protestant Bible, were prepared regardless of the cost, to stand true to God and to their consciences. That cost was the staining of the heather bells of Scotland with their blood. Shall we as sons and daughters of such men dare to be any less true in our day to the same cause.

The Session of our Church, loyal to this cause, unanimously

granted our Church Hall for the preaching of that message for which our forefathers died. The Presbytery of Down, regardless of the facts that the Session represented the people, and that the congregation wrought and gave of their money to build the hall, closed this, the property of the congregation, to the proclamation of the Gospel and suspended two Elders who refused to be mere yes-men and to join hands in such an action. This has brought to light the real character of Irish Presbyterianism.

Further, the commission of the vacancy have violated the laws of our Church by revising the poll list, which thing they had previously and publicly stated could not be done. On February 12th last, the writer openly challenged them on this issue in a letter which was read at their meeting on that date, in which was quoted paragraph 333 of the Presbyterian Code, which reads as follows: **"A poll list after being lodged with the Moderator of the Presbytery or Convenor of the vacancy, shall not be altered during the vacancy in the pastorate, unless the vacancy extends beyond twelve months; in which case the Presbytery shall have a new list of voters prepared in accordance with the preceding rules."**

In reply to this the writer received a six-page letter from the Rev Matthew Bailie, of Downpatrick, as Convenor, in which he said that the writer appeared to be in the gall of bitterness, and continued that this revision was really the result of a muddle between himself and the Presbytery, ending by stating their avowed intention not to yield one inch. It is significant that our Clerk of Session, Mr James Morrison, refused to sign the revised poll list against his conscience, and others of the Session also refused even to attend the meeting at which it was confirmed. Regardless of all this they trample on.

Facing these facts we are forced to ask ourselves the question - What is wrong with the so-called Presbyterian Church that she can act in such an unworthy manner? We go to the fountain head, the Assembly's College, and there we find the answer.

Professor Davey, Principal, and others of the professors, both in their teachings and writings deny the Truths we hold so dear, reduce the Scriptures to the level of mere human writings, make little of our Confession of Faith and Shorter Catechism, deny the very Deity and Virgin Birth of our Saviour, and place the Protestant doctrine that Christ bore our sins on the Cross on a level with the Roman Catholic doctrine of the Mass.

Even the heresy trial of 1927 failed to unseat the heretic who still has the reins of the college in his hands. To use Professor Davey's own words in Elmwood Presbyterian Church he said, "Modern scholarship has rescued the Church from the powerlessness of a propped-up religion, using the Bible as a crutch"; and that certain of the Old Testament stories are "utterly damnable."

Is this not why many of the keen Christian lads who enter the college with a sincere desire to serve Almighty God are in due course pitch-forked into our pulpits, discouraged and bewildered dupes, understanding neither what they teach, nor whereof they affirm?

The Irish Presbyterian Church took a leading part in the forming of the World Council of Churches, which betrayed the Protestant Reformation by extending a welcoming hand to the Church of Rome. You will be interested to know the Belfast Presbytery upheld those who invited Unitarian ministers to preach in their pulpits.

You say it is the church of our fathers. It is NOT the Church of our fathers. THEY were made of sterner stuff than to tolerate men who betray their trust, and violate their solemn ordination vows. Let us listen to one of these men, the sturdy Presbyterian and saintly Rutherford, who said, "Give not a hair's breadth of truth away, for it is not yours but God's."

Is this any new state of affairs? No! For generations now there has been a growing discontentment with the state of things in our Churches, and Christian people today have grave contempt for the dead and stagnant, powerless and fruitless religion of our day, and for the camouflaged modernists in our pulpits who seem to be void of any real convictions, and who read their half-baked essays with half-hearted zeal, and whose daily lives prove many of them to be mere gossip mongers, rather than soul winners. Fathers and Mothers! These men care not for the never-dying souls of your boys and girls, but rather for financial security, material comforts, and a congregation who are foolish enough to pay for the tobacco they smoke, and the worldly pleasures they pursue.

Fellow Presbyterians! What shall we do? To reform the present Church has been the desire and ambition of years, but the Irish Presbyterian Church has proved that she will adopt every measure to see that such will not happen and clear thinking Christian people are beginning to realise that the only course to pursue is to save that which is worth saving, and like Sodom and Gomorrah, leave the rest to the flames of God's wrath and judgment.

After prayerful consideration, we feel that the real need is the re-kindling of the embers which for years have been smouldering under the damping and deadening effects in our Church. In this effort I am proud to say that Crossgar has raised a leading hand, and happy to relate that she is already being joined by other congregations, now in the process of being formed. These will form what will be known as The Free Presbyterian Church of Ulster. Free because it has struggled out from under the heel and tyranny of the Church which sails under the flag of Presbyterian and because in constitution, government and worship it will be identical with that of our Presbyterian forefathers.

We believe that under the wind of heaven these embers will once again be fanned to a mighty flame all over our beloved province, and that this Free Presbyterian Body will lift again the Banner of the Cross, which has been dragged in the gutter of heresy and modernism.

This letter sets out briefly the reasons for our secession from the Church which has betrayed us, and the reason for our establishing in Crossgar a congregation of the Free Presbyterian Church of Ulster, which will by God's grace bear on the Banner of Truth carried aloft for centuries by our Presbyterian forefathers.

The Crossgar congregation of the Free Presbyterian Church of Ulster is being officially constituted on Saturday, the 17th March, in the Killyleagh Street Hall, which is being extensively renovated to serve as a temporary worshipping place. Five members of the Lissara Session will be installed as the Session of the Free Church. The opening service will be conducted on the Sabbath following (18th March) at 12 noon and 7pm with a Morning Sabbath School at 10.30. The youth organisations will be carried on under the care of the present leaders, and these will be announced at the opening services. This letter comes to you as the first official communication from the Free Church, and is approved by the following, who will constitute the Kirk Session:

James Morrison (Clerk)
WM Miscampbell
Hugh J Adams
Cecil Harvey
George K Gibson

Yours for Christ and the Truth
(signed) George K Gibson, Church Secretary.

The following scriptures you should take time to read, They illustrate the time to break down. Jeremiah 39:2 & 8; Ezekiel 33:21; Malachi 1:4 and the following illustrate the time to build up. Eccles. 2:4; Nehemiah 2: 17,18, & 20; Psalm 102:13-16; Isaiah 45:13; Isaiah 58:12, 60:10; Daniel 9:25; Amos 9:11.

A TIME TO WEEP AND A TIME TO LAUGH
ECCLESIASTES 3 V4

A TIME TO WEEP

In such a time as this there is a time to weep.

The first mention of weeping in the Bible is in Genesis 23:2, Abraham weeping over his beloved Sarah.

Abraham, who staggered not at the promise of God through unbelief, now staggers under the blow of cruel bereavement.

It seems Abraham was not there to comfort his beloved wife at her passing. The wording of verse one suggests that. 'And Sarah died in Kir-jath-arba, the same is Hebron in the land of Canaan; and Abraham came to mourn for Sarah and to weep for her.'

Not being there when our loved ones die adds sorrow to sorrow, putting extra bitterness into the already bitter cup.

No matter how much we love our dead ones we have to bury them 'out of our sight'. This is specially true in the East where corruption comes quickly to the corpse.

Yes, we all have had our weeping times and our first bereavement.

During our lifetime we have stood on life's jetty and watched our loved ones sail out across the bar. We still long for the touch of the vanished hand and the sound of the voice that is still. There is, however, no such return. We do know that those who die in Christ we only lose for 'a while'. Sweet reunion is in the offing for us all.

As I look back on the passing of my own father and mother my heart rejoices that God shed a beautiful rainbow over the valley of tears.

As I write my heart is flooded with pleasant memories. I remember my father's love for his family and his great desire that they might get the best that God had for them. He had always one great goal and objective and that was to walk in the centre of God's blessed will. Doing the will of God, for him, was a foretaste of heaven. He was a blessed man, for his love and fidelity to the Book remained unchallenged and unquestioned down through the years.

Each Lord's Day morning I would go to the House where he ministered God's precious Word. I would climb the little winding stairway to an upper room above the minister's vestry, and there I would hear my father commit his pulpit administrations and work to the Lord for that particular day. Then after that time of prayer we returned to my father's vestry where we sat until the time was ready for us to go out into the Church for the morning worship. One thing about that room always impressed me, and that was a framed picture of the great C. H. Spurgeon bearing his own autograph. My father was a Spurgeon man. He walked in the tradition of the Puritans, and he looked upon Spurgeon as one of the greatest Puritans of them all, summing up in his sermons the quintessence of the whole Puritan theology.

I have happy memories of my father in the pulpit pleading with souls as one who must give account; strong in his denunciation of evil, never slothful in business but ever fervent in spirit, serving the Lord. I think as a preacher he excelled most in the evangelistic field. It was my joy and privilege to attend many of his evangelistic campaigns in tents, in barns, in homes, in orange halls and in church buildings. There he stood forth as God's ambassador, as though God did beseech men by him, he prayed them in Christ's stead to be reconciled to God. His zeal was unbounded. His prayers were an inspiration and his preaching had upon it the unction of heaven. Many rose up in those services and embraced the Saviour whom he lifted up with all the fervency of spiritual might. No doubt on the great judgment day those precious souls, who through my father's ministry were seals of God's approval, will rise up to bless the Name of the Saviour and to rejoice that God ever sent among them a man called James Kyle Paisley. My indebtedness to my father cannot be expressed. It is beyond evaluation. He taught me how to get my priorities right. He ingrained into me the great teaching of the Saviour, that a man's life consisteth not in the abundance of the things which he possesses. He showed me that the secret of the ministry was neither popularity nor conformity to ecclesiastical procedures and formalities but rather a conformity to God's Word and a fidelity to the Holy Book and the Holy Gospel. His righteous indignation against Romanism, modernistic apostasy and ecumenism put within me a holy hatred for those systems that would tear the crown from the brow of the Saviour and seek to exalt man as the author and co-author of his own redemption. My father was zealous for the glory of the Lord. He battled hard in his day against the floodtide of apostasy that was then starting to flow throughout our Province. Until the end he remained unwavering in his first love for Christ and his fervency in opposing all that God was against and standing for all that God was for. His ministry was a lonely one. He walked the road of separation and in many senses a road of isolation because of the attitude of many of his brethren, but he walked with the Lord in the light of His Word.

His partnership with my mother was a blessed one. They both saw eye to eye in the things of God, and they both longed to see the coming of men and women into the kingdom of God's dearly beloved Son. Their partnership in the home was carried over into partnership in the field of evangelism and in the work of God's House. They both strove together mightily for the furtherance of the Gospel. Now they are gone from us, but thank God, their works do follow them. The battles, the victories, the sacrifices and the determination of a man and a woman of God doing their bit for God in their own day and generation is an inspiration to me today.

May we, spurred on by their example, walk the same path of fidelity to God's Truth and be able to say, as they could have well said at the end of the journey, 'We have fought a good fight, we have finished the course, we have kept the faith.'

What though the arm of conquering death
Does God's own House invade,
What though the prophet and the priest
Be numbered with the dead;

Though earthly shepherds dwell in dust
The aged and the young.
The watchful eye in darkness closed
In mute, the instructive tongue.

The Eternal Shepherd still survives
You comfort to impart;
His eye still guides us and His voice
Still animates our heart.

Though I am with you, saith the Lord,
My church shall safe abide,
For I will ne'er forsake my own
Whose souls in me confide.

Through every scene of life and death
This promise is our trust,
And this shall be our children's song
When we are cold in dust.

A TIME TO LAUGH

The first time that the word *"weep"* occurs in the Bible is in the record of Abraham weeping on the death of his wife, Sarah.

Interestingly, the first time that the word *"laughing"* occurs in the Bible is in the record of Abraham laughing the laugh of faith at the promise of God about Isaac Sarah's son.

There are two scriptures which need to be placed side by side .

1. Genesis 17: 15-17 : *"And God said unto Abraham, As for Sarai thy wife, thou shalt not call her name Sarai, but Sarah shall her name be. And I will bless her, and give thee a son also of her: yea, I will bless her, and she shall be a mother of nations; kings of people shall be of her. Then Abraham fell upon his face, and laughed, and said in his heart, Shall a child be born*

unto him that is an hundred years old? and shall Sarah, that is ninety years old, bear?"

2. Genesis 18:9-12: *"And they said unto him, Where is Sarah thy wife? And he said, Behold, in the tent. And he said, I will certainly return unto thee according to the time of life; and lo, Sarah thy wife shall have a son. And Sarah heard it in the tent door, which was behind him. Now Abraham and Sarah were old and well stricken in age; and it ceased to be with Sarah after the manner of women. Therefore Sarah laughed within herself saying, After I am waxed old shall I have pleasure, my lord being old also?"*

They both have reference to laughing.

The first one which is the first mention in the whole Bible, is - **the laugh of faith.**

Abram in verse three of the chapter fell on his face. He needed to. God had not appeared to him since his taking of Hagar on the urging of Sarai and the birth of Ishmael.

Ishmael was born when Abram was 86 years old (Genesis 16:16). For four years God had not appeared to Abram.

When he was ninety years God appeared once again. Then Abram fell on his face. He fell in penitence because he had done wrong to go Sarai's way instead of God's way for an heir, His chosen seed.

Another ten years must pass before that seed would be born and Sarah the princess, not Hagar the slave girl, would be the mother. Abraham was one hundred years old when Isaac was born (Genesis 21:5).

After Abram repented God changed his name to Abraham. He did that by putting into his name Abram the Hebrew letter Heth = H (the fifth letter of the Hebrew alphabet) and making it Abraham. By a similar insertion he changed his wife's name Sarai to Sarah. Five in scripture is the number of grace, so by the adding of grace a new dimension was entered in God's dealing with Abram.

Notice that Abraham fell on his face the second time (verse 17). This was in gratitude. He laughed for joy. He fell on his face overcome with happiness. Literally the Hebrew reads, *"Abraham was joyful"*.

This must have been the incident which our Lord Jesus spoke of in John 8:56: *"Your father Abraham rejoiced to see my day: and he saw it, and was glad."*

This was the joy of faith. Romans 4:19-22: *"And being not weak in faith, he considered not his own body now dead, when he was about an hundred years old, neither yet the deadness of Sara's womb: He staggered not at the promise of God through unbelief; but was strong in faith, giving glory to God. And being fully persuaded that, what he had promised, he was able also to perform. And therefore it was imputed to him for right-eousness."*

Notice now the contrast. In Genesis 18:11 Sarah had a different sort of a laugh. It was not outward but inward. It was the laugh of unbelief. In verse 15 she denied that she laughed, bringing the Lord's rebuke. Verse15: *"Then Sarah denied, saying, I laughed not; for she was afraid. And he said, Nay; but thou didst laugh."*

Now Abraham laughed openly. He fell on his face. He was joyful. Then he said in his heart. *"Shall a child be born unto him that is one hundred years old and shall Sarah that is ninety bear?'* God had evidently told Abraham that in ten years time the promise would be made good, although it is not specifically mentioned.

He staggered not at the promises of God through (Romans 4:20) unbelief but was strong in faith giving glory to God,

In Genesis 21:2 we have the confirmation that God told Abraham that he would be one hundred years old when his son would be born. Abraham's joy was outward and his inward meditation was stamped by faith.

Sarah's laughter was hidden and was one of derision and her inward meditation was unbelieving.

Happy Abraham! Miserable Sarah!

God cannot deny Himself. He is faithful that promised. He also will do it.

The next reference in Genesis to Sarah laughing is not secretive and scornful but public and believing.

Genesis 21: 1-7: *"And the Lord visited Sarah as he had said, and the Lord did unto Sarah as he had spoken. For Sarah conceived, and bare Abraham a son in his old age, at the set time of which God had spoken to him. And Abraham called the name of his son that was born unto him, whom Sarah bare to him, Issac. And Abraham circumcised his son Isaac being eight days old, as God had commanded him. And Abraham was an hundred years old when his son Isaac was born unto him.*

And Sarah said, God hath made me to laugh, so that all that hear will laugh with me. And she said, Who would have said unto Abraham, that Sarah should have given children suck? for I have born him a son in his old age."

God who sits in the heavens laughs and has all unbelievers in derision.

In 1951 a prominent minister came to me and rebuked me.

He said, "Who do you think you are, a lad of 25 years challenging the other churches and daring to set up another denomination? You cannot succeed. You are doomed to failure. A few years and your nonsense and folly will be exposed."

That same man, who at that time served a church outside the ecumenical movement, went to England, was ordained into the Church of England and joined up with a Church that had all the apostasy of the Antichrist in it. His neighbouring clergy were mass-mongers, 'apeists of Rome'.

No wonder he hated my stand and the stand of the Free Presbyterian Church.

Every time I open yet another new Free Presbyterian Church I think of that brother.

Of course I and my brethren couldn't do anything, but our God could and has and can. I learned to laugh along with God and what laughs I have had with the victories of faith and the confounding of the enemies of the gospel.

God's people and servants have always been God's laugh at the devil and the devil's crowd.

Abel was God's everlasting laugh at Cain the first unitarian.

Cain thought he would exile the blood theology from off the whole earth and that "un bloody" unitarianism would reign unchallenged and unchallengable. What a laugh! The dead spoke and the very blood which he thought he had destroyed forever cried out loudly to God. Yes, and God heard it and Cain became the vagabond and exile.

Enoch was God's laugh at the filthy age in which he lived. He disappeared. They sent out search parties for him but "he was not found" (Heb. 12:4).

They thought he was a fool, but what fools they were looking for Enoch while Enoch looked down from heaven upon their folly.

Noah was God's laugh at the earth filled with violence and vice.

What jokes were cracked at the old man building a great ship miles from the sea, to save the beasts of the field and the fowls of the air! Crackpot!

What a laugh when Noah sailed to safety and the intelligentsia sank in terror into the depths! I would prefer, like Noah, the company of the animals and the fowls to theirs.

Abraham was God's laugh at every generation of mankind that has and will occupy this earth. He was promised a seed which would inherit the heaven and the earth. When he was 99 and his wife was 89 no seed had yet been born. But God fulfilled all His promises to this man. Indeed he was THE FRIEND OF GOD.

Today both his spiritual seed and natural seed are before us doing exactly what God said they would do. Abraham, God's laugh at all generations of mankind.

Young Joseph was God's laugh at his arrogant brethren. What a laugh - from valued at one old pound (20 pieces of silver) to being Prime Minister of the greatest world power of the day.

Baby Moses - what a laugh was he against the same world power. Made heir of Egypt he turned from Egypt's riches and chose rather the reproaches of Christ. He waited from he was 40 until he was 80 before he entered into his life's work. He led three million slaves out of bondage to liberty. What a laugh when the murderous Pharaoh had to swim for it but never made the shore, while Moses on dry land celebrated the final victory.

Joshua was God's laugh at the Hittites, the Amorites, the Canaanites, the Perizzites, the Hivites, the Jebusites and all the other Arabian knights.

He tumbled down the walls of their cities and carried out a conquering occupation unparalleled in military history, aided by the hornets as his unique guerilla fighters. What a laugh on the nations of Canaan!

Rahab was God's laugh on proud Jericho. A harlot became God's heroine and found a place as an ancestress of the Lord Jesus in the great genealogy.

That loud laugh of God re-echoes around the globe until this day.

"And what shall I more say? for the time would fail me to tell of Gideon, and of Barak, and of Samson, and of Jephthae; of David also, and Samuel, and of the prophets: Who through faith subdued kingdoms, wrought right-eousness, obtained promises, stopped the mouths of lions, Quenched the violence of fire, escaped the edge of the sword, out of weakness were made strong, waxed valiant in fight, turned to flight the armies of the aliens.

Women received their dead raised to life again: and others were tortured, not accepting deliverance; that they might obtain a better resurrection: And others had trial of cruel mockings and scourgings, yea, moreover of bonds and imprisonment: They were stoned, they were sawn asunder, were tempted, were slain with the sword: they wandered about in sheepskins and goatskins; being destitute, afflicted, tormented; (Of whom the world was not worthy:) they wandered in deserts, and in mountains, and in dens and caves of the earth. And these all, having obtained a good report through faith, received not the promise: God having provided some better thing for us, that they without us should not be made perfect." (Heb 11:32-40)

All God's laughs have wicked sinners in derision.

Turning back again to Isaac it is worth while to recall that the name *Isaac* in the Hebrew means literally *let him laugh.*

So Isaac actually laughed along with his mother. Isaac was born to laughter and so is the child of God.

The God of heaven orders *"Let him laugh,"* and laugh he did.

Laughter is the character of God and every child of His walking in the keeping of His commandments.

"Let him laugh" was what God ordered for Isaac on Mount Moriah, and with what laughter and joy Abraham returned with Isaac to Sarah, an Isaac delivered from the wrath to come.

What a laugh arises within our souls when we view the glory of the Lamb of God in substitution for His believing people as they come into the experience of sins forgiven.

Then was our mouth filled with laughter, the laughter of God.

What a laugh arises within our souls when God turns on His enemies and makes them as dust, when the trumpet of God sounds and the Lord God giveth us the victory.

"When the Lord turned again the captivity of Zion, we were like them that dream. Then was our mouth filled with laughter, and our tongue with singing: then said the Lord among the heathen, The Lord hath done great things for them. The Lord hath done great things for us; whereof we are glad. Turn again our captivity, O Lord, as the streams in the south. They that sow in tears shall reap in joy. He that goeth forth and weepeth, bearing precious seed, shall doubtless come again with rejoicing, bringing his sheaves with him." (Psalm 126:1-6).

Oh to serve such a God with holy mouth, and tell forth exceedingly and fully the praises of such a God Who has called us out of darkness into His most marvellous light.

How often we have had this experience of knowing how God has confounded the enemies of His people.

In Armagh, the city of my birth, I conducted an evangelistic tent campaign. God was pleased to bless His Holy Gospel. Many were converted to Christ and those who had sat too long in the apostasy decided that the time had come to separate from the great religious evil of our day and go outside the camp to bear reproach for Christ their Saviour.

A second tent had to be erected to hold the crowds attending the services. The man who owned the field had no objection to us continuing to use the tent for church services on his property.

After we held our first Lord's Day morning service we were ordered off the ground. The apostate church had decided we had to be shifted. The owner of the ground was leaned on and so the congregation just formed was homeless after its first Lord's Day service.

But *"He that sitteth in the heavens shall laugh, the Lord shall have them in derision."*

Here was I and I had just formed a church of some 50 to 60 people and they and I were on the street.

When I tried to rent a public hall all public halls were barred against us.

The only one thing we could do was to pray and pray we did, as the mounting tide of opposition rose against us in the city of Armagh.

Then I received a telephone call from the Church of God at Belfast indicating that they had a piece of ground on the Mall, right in the centre of the city. It was situated between the Gospel Hall and the First Presbyterian Church. They offered that ground to me if it would be of immediate use for the erection of a portable building.

It was now Tuesday.

On Wednesday I bought a portable hall from a Brethren preacher and the erection of that hall started to take place.

I did not apply for planning permission for I knew it would be refused. I knew also that I could erect the building and if the planning authorities sought to have me remove it they would have to go to court. That would take time and at least give breathing space to the fledgling congregation.

On Thursday I received a telephone call from my workers in Armagh who were on the site erecting the portable hall, to say that the Official Unionist Chairman of the Town Council, the Town Clerk of the Council and the Chief of Police in Armagh, the District Inspector of the Royal Ulster Constabulary were on the site demanding the work would cease. My workers said that I needed to come down immediately and see what I could do. I said, "give me an hour and I'll be there."

I rang my lawyer to get advice. He informed me what I already knew that only a court order could make me remove the building. He instructed me to tell the three intruders, Council Chairman, Town Clerk and Town Chief of Police that they were trespassing on my property and if they were not off immediately my men would put them off it.

I got to Armagh and the three bully boys of the apostasy arrived. I told the Chief of Police, who was a Methodist, that I wondered what had come over him because instead of keeping the law he was breaking it and helping the Town Clerk and the Council Chairman to act unlawfully.

The Council Chairman who was a leading Orangeman, thundered that he personally would see to it that under no circumstances at any time would a Free Presbyterian Church ever get planning permission in Armagh.

I made a note of that threat and told him he would be called to answer for it when the courts would adjudicate on the matter. I reminded him that he had neither the power nor the authority to do what he threatened. I would see to it, if I never did anything else, that he would be indicted, charged and exposed before the proper lawful authorities.

I then told these three agents of the apostasy to leave my property. I told them that they were trespassers and if they were not off in three minutes my men would assist them to keep the law.

The Chief of Police was the first to break. He acknowledged it was a matter for the courts, that they were in law trespassing and he advised his fellow agents to leave the site with him. In a flaming rage the Council Chairman left, vowing that no Free Presbyterian Church would ever be erected in the town.

On the Lord's Day the building was opened. God worked and precious souls were delivered savingly in that meeting house which Church and State tried to close.

The three agents of apostasy did not prosper. The Chief of Police retired, the Town Clerk ceased to hold his appointment and the leading Orangeman and Official Unionist Council Chairman who swore that no Free Presbyterian Church would ever be built in Armagh fell a tragic victim to IRA violence and was brutally murdered by those republicans that he refused to oppose. That, however, is a story for another day.

We had a temporary meeting house but that was only a very short term gain.

The authorities were moving against us. I looked for ground and then one day standing near the temporary meeting house on the Mall, I looked over the Armagh prison roof and saw a large piece of ground on one of the seven hills of this ancient city of St Patrick.

I enquired who owned it. It belonged to a local butcher. I made my way prayerfully to his business premises. That hill, higher than the two hills which site the Church of Ireland Cathedral and the Roman Catholic Cathedral respectively, was the ideal site left vacant since creation's morning for the Free Presbyterian Church which was never to be built, according to our enemies.

The butcher received me most graciously but told me I must bring him the name of my solicitor and £1,000 immediately, as there were others interested.

I made an appointment for that very afternoon and then called on a friend of mine who was good for £1,000 on loan. Having secured the money and given my friend my promise of speedy repayment I ate a hearty lunch (and I could do that in those days) and waited for the afternoon.

I was anxious in case there might be some hitch, that something might change the circumstances. It seemed after all the bother and the fiercest opposition that it was too easy.

Then faith's sun came out and lightened my way and I began to laugh. God's laugh in the heaven had become contagious. *"He that sitteth in heavens shall laugh, the Lord shall have them in derision."*

Today a beautiful church building occupies that site and a large congregation worships within its walls.

There is a time to laugh in such a time as this.

That was the day when God gave the apostasy a black eye.

A TIME TO MOURN AND A TIME TO DANCE
ECCLESIASTES 3 V 4

Ulster has been plunged into the deepest depths of mourning over the past years of terrorism, initiated by the so-called Irish Republican Army and then spread through counter reaction of so-called loyalists.

The depths of that mourning for innocent victims on both sides is of the greatest intensity. Ulster weeping for her sons and daughters and would not be comforted because they are not.

I know, for I have been in vast numbers of homes both Protestant and Roman Catholic in their day of deepest anguish and in their hour of utter darkness.

I know what it is to lay one hand on a curly headed boy and the other on the head of a curly headed girl and know they will grow up without any real remembrance of a noble father and gentle mother. There is nothing that tears at the heartstrings like that. It would fill a book if I related the many experiences which I have had in my pastoral ministry in the presence of death. I am only going to mention two homes that through the troubles were plunged into the depth of this suffering, sorrow and sacrifice.

They are typical of many but I simply chose these two because of their spiritual connection.

The first I will not name because what I must say might offend the relations still living whose sympathies may not tally with mine.

He was a fine man in his forties or perhaps a little older. He was a believer in Christ and had experienced the transformation of the new birth. He loved the Word of God, the Reformed Faith and the old time Protestant religion.

He was a Presbyterian born and bred and a lover of the church of his fathers. He became an elder in a local Presbyterian congregation.

He grieved the departure of Gospel light from so many pulpits of the Presbyterian churches. He had his eyes opened to the destructive principles of the ecumenical movement and the Romeward trends gaining more and more ground within Irish Presbyterianism.

He mourned over, and protested against, the denials of the Faith, especially the virgin birth of Christ and precious redeeming Blood of the Saviour.

He came to see that there was only one way for him and that was to separate from that which had separated itself from Christ. A Christian church, as Dr Cooke so plainly put it, cannot be both Trinitarian and Unitarian. A stand must be made. We must declare on whose side we are.

This dear brother fervently cried out, "I am on the Lord's side, Saviour I am Thine."

So he obeyed God rather than men and resigned his eldership and membership in the Irish Presbyterian Church and became a Free Presbyterian. In those early days the Free Presbyterian Church was described by one prominent Irish Presbyterian minister as a "mad man's asylum". This dear brother's wife and family did not agree with him, opposition was kindled against him and he was persecuted for obeying the Holy Scripture.

He had made up his mind. The Lord had called. He had obeyed God and through ill report he now gladly bore reproach for the Saviour who loved him and gave Himself for him.

He was a police officer, a member of the Royal Ulster Constabulary, a true patriot and lover of his Province and country.

When the attacks on the police commenced in Londonderry he was one of the first to be drafted in to keep order in the republican and Roman Catholic Bogside. Like hundreds of his colleagues he was drenched with petrol bombs and set alight in order to put him out of action and if possible, out of this world.

He endured, with his colleagues, such attacks night after night and day after day, with just a few hours of sleep each twenty four hours then back to the same bombings and burnings.

The Northern Ireland Government under O'Neill handed the police over to republican terror and would not permit them to use the necessary force to break these republican thugs and would-be murderers. Their hands were tied behind their backs as Terence O'Neill posed as a man of peace and reconciliation. The police became the sacrifice freely offered on the altar of political appeasement.

O'Neill was afraid of Prime Minister Wilson and would not commit himself to the task of smashing the republicans who were determined to smash Ulster.

Ulster was defeated, not by frontal assault but by treachery. She was wounded to death in the house of her friends.

At the end of a gruelling time of front line duty in this terrible and indescribable terror situation, he returned to his home a broken man. Cancer came on as a result and the sentence was death.

How sad to see my dear brother in such a state! What a heartbreaking experience to see him who was once the picture of life and vitality now but a mere skelf of his former self.

But in his spirit, he was unbroken. The tabernacle of clay was smashed. The earthly house was dissolving every minute but the inward man was renewed every day. The triumph of Christ who is the resurrection and life was winning the victory.

Soon, thank God, the heavenly trumpet sounded, the divine summons was served and another Valiant for Truth passed over to the other side in glorious victory.

He had fought a good fight both physically and spiritually and the crown of life was laid up for him in the everlasting home of his Father's house.

His sacrifice and bravery, like so many others, was unchronicled and unmarked. He died without tribute except by his family and those who loved him and by his colleagues who had witnessed his courage and heroism.

In the even greater battle he fought and won with the end time apostasy, his deeds are chronicled in the records of God forever. His name is on the Saviour's Roll of Honour. He will not go unmentioned or unrewarded before heaven and earth and hell in God's great Reckoning Day. The highest honour in God's list will undoubtedly be his SWD (the Saviour's Well Done).

Thank God I'll be there to see him receive that honour of all honours.

John Bunyan's words on the passing of Mr. Valiant-for-Truth are most appropriate to our brother's passing:

> "After this it was noised abroad, that Mr. Valiant-for-Truth was taken with a summons by the same post as the other; and had this for a token that the summons was true, "That his pitcher was broken at the fountain." When he understood it, he called for his friends, and told them of it. Then, said he, I am going to my Father's; and though with great difficulty I am got hither, yet now I do not repent me of all the trouble I have been at to arrive where I am. My sword I give to him that shall succeed me in my pilgrimage, and my courage and skill to him that can get it. My marks and scars I carry with me, to be a witness for me, that I have fought His battles who now will be my rewarder. When the day that he must go hence was come, many accompanied him to the river side, into which as he went he said, "Death, where is thy sting?" And as he went down deeper, he said, "Grave, where is thy victory?" So he passed over, and all the trumpets sounded for him on the other side."

Yes his passing and its circumstances, in such a time as this, is a time to mourn. Ah yes! Weeping will endure during the night of our sojourn here below but joy cometh in the morning. We say "Goodnight" in tears. We will say "Good morning" in joy.

The second case is that of a much younger man.

Young Fred Starrett was born on 21st June, 1965. He was saved by grace on the 18th July, 1979. He was an earnest worker in the Every Home Crusade. He taught Sabbath School in our Ballybeen Sunday School. He served part-time in the Ulster Defence Regiment.

He was murdered by an IRA bomb along with his fellow comrade in the Regiment, James Cummins.

Fred's father, whom Fred earnestly prayed for, found Christ after his son's funeral service. He went to meet his son some eight years ago. His dear mother, Susan, and his loving sister Violet are still with us and constantly in our prayers.

John Bunyan in his immortal dream speaks thus of the passing of Stand-fast. It is a fitting obituary to young Fred.

"I see myself now at the end of my journey, my toilsome days are ended. I am going now to see that head that was crowned with thorns, and that face that was spit upon for me.

I have formerly lived by hearsay and faith: but now I go where I shall live by sight, and shall be with HIm in whose company I delight myself.

I have loved to hear my Lord spoken of; and wherever I have seen the print of His shoe in the earth, there I have coveted to set my foot too.

His name has been to me as a civet-box; yea, sweeter than all perfumes. His voice to me has been most sweet; and His countenance I have more desired than they that have most desired the light of the sun. His word I did use to gather for my food, and for antidotes against my faintings. "He has held me, and I have kept me from mine iniquites; yea, my steps hath he strengthened in His way."

Now, while he was thus in discourse, his countenance changed, his strong man bowed under him; and after he had said, Take me, for I come unto Thee, he ceased to be seen of them.

But glorious it was to see how the open region was filled with horses and chariots, with trumpeters and pipers, with singers and players on stringed instruments, to welcome the Pilgrims as they went up, and followed one another in at the beautiful gate of the city."

Today we have our tears, tomorrow we will share Fred's triumph. Farewell, dear Fred, we shall meet you in the morning.

A TIME TO DANCE

In 1966 Rev John Wylie and Rev Ivan Foster, then a student ministers of the Free Presbyterian Church, and I were imprisoned in the Crumlin Road Prison for three months because we refused to be bound over to keep the peace.

Terence O'Neill, the Prime Minister, thought he had won a great victory. The ecumenists in the Presbyterian Church, the Church of Ireland and the Methodist Church with their allies in Rome and in the other smaller denominations infiltrated by ecumenism, rejoiced.

The obituary notice of "Paisleyism", as the Belfast Telegraph called it, was written. The Free Presbyterian Church was finished. So all the clerical corncrakes sounded off. It was a heyday in the camp of apostasy. However, for God's people the days to dance were at hand, though totally blind priests and partially blind persons could not see it.

Throughout the country my wife and others addressed rallies attended by tens of thousands of people. The press played down these rallies they are still at the same game - but at Cookstown their smoke screen was blown when it was established irrefutably that 10,000 were in attendance at one such rally.

Thousands of people from all over the world wrote to the Queen. In the Public Records Office in Belfast there is the record of those letters.

Meanwhile prominent fundamentalist leaders from all over the world visited Ravenhill Free Presbyterian Church and the Crumlin Road Prison. O'Neill began to shake. The ecumenical leaders came in for strong criticism. It was evident two laws were at work in Northern Ireland, one exceedingly soft on Roman Catholic republicans and the other exceedingly rough of Protestant Unionists. In the meantime my wife fought a by-election in Duncairn Ward for the

City Council and gave the O'Neillites a run for their political money. She was afterwards elected at the top of the poll for St. George's Ward.

Meanwhile a spiritual work was going on in the churches. New congregations were springing up. I have mentioned them before.

Many of our political supporters saw through the deceit, compromise and treachery of the ecumenical clergy and came to various church services and got gloriously converted. Drunkards, gamblers and hard men of the world were gloriously converted. What a joy it was to meet them when we came out of prison. I have already mentioned the quantum leap in our church membership.

Then came the resignation of Prime Minister O'Neill and a General Election for the Northern Ireland Parliament. I stood against O'Neill, who had never fought an election in his whole political career. I came a close second. His political death knell had sounded. One ballot box which was not satisfactorily accounted for would perhaps have made the difference. However, in twelve months O'Neill quit and in the by-election I took his seat. At the same time Rev William Beattie took the South Antrim seat. To God be the glory.

In such a time as this there is a time to dance.

The impossible made possible. The unthinkable became actuality. The irresistable was smashed to smithereens.

When David brought up the ark to Zion it was a time to dance (II Samuel 6:14) For Michal, Saul's daughter and David's first wife, it was a time which caused her dancing to cease forever. The praising of God was in the dance (Psalm 149:3, Psalm 150:4), not mixed lustful dancing of the world but single dancing of each sex separately.

"Then shall the virgin rejoice in the dance, both young men and old together: for I will turn their mourning into joy and will comfort them and make them rejoice from their sorrow. And I will satiate the soul of the priests with fatness and My people shall be satisfied with my goodness, saith the Lord. (Jer. 31:13-14).

A TIME TO CAST AWAY STONES AND A TIME TO GATHER STONES
ECCLESIASTES 3 V 4

A TIME TO CAST AWAY STONES

The casting away of stones is clearly the launching of an attack on those things which hinder the work of God and the forward movement of the Cause of God and Truth.

This is illustrated in the Scriptures.

"And he fenced it, and gathered out the stones thereof, and planted it with the choicest vine, and built a tower in the midst of it, and also made a winepress therein: and he looked that it should bring forth grapes, and it brought forth wild grapes." (Isaiah 5:2).

Note the expression *"gathered out the stones thereof"*. The stones were detrimental to the growth of the vine, because they prevented the roots from to penetrating the soil.

I remember in County Tyrone after we prepared the ground for sowing of the corn we gathered the stones out of the field that was to be sowed. Christ, in His parable of the sower warns of the fruitlessness of stoney places (Matthew 13:5 and 20-22, Mark 4:5-6 and 5:16-17).

There has to be a casting away of the stones. The seed, we are told by Christ, is the Word of God (Mark 4:14). Those who will not give room to the Word of God must be cast out. In this day whole battalions of the apostate churches oppose and resist the Word of God. In their training colleges the Word of God is attacked and its eternal truths denied.

Principal JE Davey who destroyed the orthodoxy of Irish Presbyterianism left on record a blasphemous attack on the Word of God both Incarnate and Inspired.

In such a time as this it is surely time to cast away such stones.

The Irish Presbyterian Church in its highest court, the General Assembly, endorsed his teachings as the doctrine of the church on these subjects by and approved Dr. Davey's justification of the same.

No wonder we put Davey's writings to the flame to draw attention to their vile blasphemies and hellish insults on the Son of God.

One of the Irish Presbyterian nitwits demonstrated the lack of grey matter between his ears when he likened us to Rome burning the Bible. We tried as patiently as we could to instill some light into this poor ecclesiastical imbecile by pointing out that Rome sought to burn every Bible ever printed in order to keep them from the people. In contrast, Luther burned the Papal Bull of excommunication to highlight and expose the Papal dictatorship. We had adopted Luther's methods. It was Davey and his infidel ilk who acted like Rome and tried to destroy the Bible.

Thank God for those who joined us in such a time as this to cast away the stones which sought to destroy the Word of God. God give more power to our elbows to ever engage in this God honouring work.

Davey is forgotten but the Word of God, which he so hellishly attacked, is not bound. God has indeed *"magnified His Word above all His name."* (Psalm 138:2).

TIME TO GATHER STONES TOGETHER

After clearing the building site we must take care how we gather stones together to build thereon. In many ways, other men laboured and we have entered into their labours.

I salute the memory of my own dear father who brought on 1st August, 1946 my ordination charge. He raised the battle standard against the apostasy in the early days and sounded the trumpet as a faithful watchman on the walls of Zion. The following words which he quoted on that occasion have remained with me.

The Mighty Ordination

From the glory and the gladness,
From His secret place,
From the rapture of His presence,
From His radiant face.
Christ, the Son of God, hath sent me
Through the midnight lands,
Mine the mighty ordination
Of the pierced hands.

Mine the message grand and glorious,
Strange, unsealed surprise,
That the goal is God's beloved,
Christ in paradise.

Hear me, weary men and women,
Sinners dead in sin;
I am come from Heaven to tell you
Of the love within;
Not alone of God's great pathway
Leading up to Heaven;
Not alone how you may enter,
Stainless and forgiven.

But I tell you I have seen Him,
God's beloved Son,
From His lips have learnt the mystery,
He and I are one.
There, as knit into the Body,
Every joint and limb,
We, His ransomed, His beloved,
We are one with Him.

The tide of "modernism", falsely so-called, was running in full tide. It seemed that religiously it was carrying all before it.

At his funeral I was able to pay him this tribute:

> "Farewell, dear father, thou wast a beloved partner and thou art now united with thy loved one, my mother. Thou wast a loving and kind parent, and thy sons and daughter and grandchildren rise up this day and call thee blessed. Thou was a true patriot, a lover of thy country, a defender of its soil, an interceder for its people. Above all, thou wast a zealous preacher of the gospel of the Free Grace of God. The many souls saved under your ministry, some now in heaven and many still on the way, will shine as stars in your crown for ever and ever. Thou wast a faithful pastor and didst tend diligently the flock of God, over which the Holy Ghost made thee an overseer. Dear father, beloved partner, gracious parent, true patriot, zealous preacher, faithful pastor, thy race is run, thy crown is won. Your Bible is my Bible. Your God is my God. Your Saviour is my Saviour. And blessed be the Name of Jesus, your heaven will be my heaven some day."

In Deut 27:1-8 we read these words: "*And Moses with the elders of Israel commanded the people, saying, Keep all the commandments which I command you this day. And it shall be on the day when ye shall pass over Jordan unto the land which the Lord thy God giveth thee, that thou shalt set thee up great stones, and plaister them with plaister. And thou shalt write upon them all the words of this law, when thou art passed over, that thou mayest go in unto the land which the Lord thy God giveth thee, a land that floweth with milk and honey; as the Lord God of thy fathers hath promised thee. Therefore it shall be when ye be gone over Jordan, that ye shall set up these stones, which I command you this day, in mount Ebal, and thou shalt plaister them with plaister. And there shalt thou build an altar unto the Lord thy God, an altar of stones: thou shalt not lift up any iron tool upon them. Thou shalt build the altar of the Lord thy God of whole stones: and thou shalt offer burnt offerings thereon unto the Lord thy God; And thou shalt offer peace offerings, and shalt eat there, and rejoice before the Lord thy God. And thou shalt write upon the stones all the words of this law very plainly.*"

The gathering of stones at the entrance door to the promised land.

The gathering of stones was for the building of the altar, for there is no way we can enter the promised land if we do not gather the stones for the altar. Then you will notice that upon this altar was placed the sacrifice of the burnt offering and the sacrifice of the peace offering. There must be judgment before there is peace. The word of God states clearly 'first purity, then peace'. We have an attempt today to sponsor peace movements and peace processes built upon lies, deceit and wickedness, but they cannot stand, because first there must come purity and then peace.

Then notice in the gathering of the stones there was to be written the law of the Lord. On the plaster that held the stones together the ten commandments of God were to be written very plainly so that there would be no doubt of a single letter. In other words, every 'i' was to be dotted and every 't' crossed. Today we need to gather the stones, we need to plaster them, and write upon them plainly the whole truth of God. There must be no diminution of the truth, and there must be no addition to the truth. It must stand as the Lord has written it, for God says, 'What I have written, I have written, and cursed be the man who takes from it or adds to it.' We must get back to the word of God. The entrance to the life of joy is the entrance at the altar of sacrifice, the blood-shedding of the burnt offering and the peace offering, and we must hear and bow to and obey and practice the law of God.

Then we are told we are to be joyful. Look at verse 7: 'And thou shalt offer peace offerings and shalt eat there and rejoice before the 'Lord'. On the basis of blood-shedding and reconciliation, on the basis of the exaltation of, and submission to, God's word there comes joy unspeakable and full of glory to the hearts of those that walk in obedience.

When we walk with the Lord,
In the light of His word,
What a glory He sheds on our way.
While we do His good will
He abides with us still,
And with all who will trust and obey.

In Joshua chapter four we have more gathering of stones. Here we have the gathering of twelve stones from the depths of the Jordan. Joshua 4:3. *"And command ye them, saying, Take you hence out of the midst of Jordan, out of the place where the priests' feet stood firm, twelve stones, and ye shall carry them over with you, and leave them in the lodging place, where ye shall lodge this night."*

Verse 8, *"And the children of Israel did so as Joshua commanded, and took up twelve stones out of the midst of Jordan, as the Lord spake unto Joshua, according to the number of the tribes of the children of Israel, and carried them over with them unto the place where they lodged, and laid them down there."*

Verse 20, *"And those twelve stones, which they took out of Jordan, did Joshua pitch in Gilgal."*

So here we have the gathering of stones out of the river. Now Jordan is a type of death, it is the river of separation that divides the wilderness from the promised land, and here we find that Joshua is commanded to gather stones, 'the place where the priests' feet stood firm.' Thank God there is a place where the great High Priest, the one who is the antitype of all the Levitical priesthood and Aaronic priesthood, who is the antitype of the ark that these priests carried across Jordan, the Lord Jesus Christ, stood firm for us at Calvary, and though Satan bruised His heel, the Lord Jesus Christ with bleeding feet stood firm to redeem His people. That great victory is celebrated by taking the stones, the foundations upon which the priests stood, and putting them as a marker on the other side of the water. Thank God we have those great twelve foundation stones of the great Cross-work of the Lord Jesus Christ, and continually we should be erecting these stones so that all might know that the preaching of the Cross is to them that perish foolishness, but to them who are saved it is indeed the power of God.

We turn now to 1 Samuel chapter 17, verse 40: *"And he took his staff in his hand, and chose him five smooth stones out of the brook, and put them in a shepherd's bag which he had, even in a scrip; and his sling was in his hand: and he drew near to the Philistine."* Verse 49 of the same chapter: *"And David put his hand in his bag, and took thence a stone, and slang it, and smote the Philistine in his forehead, that the stone sunk into his forehead; and he fell upon his face to the earth. So David prevailed over the Philistine with a sling and with a stone, and smote the Philistine and slew him."*

GATHERED STONES

Young David gathered five stones. Many questions have been asked about these five stones - why five stones? One thing is sure, that this battle with Goliath was a type of a greater battle which the Lord Jesus Christ would fight with the Goliath of Hell. When the Lord Jesus fought the Devil at His temptation, you will remember that he used three quotations, and all three quotations were from the book of Deuteronomy. They were the one stone which destroyed him that had the power of death, that is to say, the Devil, and delivered those who through fear of death, were all their lifetime subject to bondage. It is interesting to note that Goliath of Gath had four brothers, and someone has said that he took four stones, one for each of the brothers, so they could avenge his death. One thing is sure, and that is that David not only used the one stone but he brought it back with him , for he cut off Goliath's head, and in that head was the stone that killed him. The other four stones were still in the scrip, and so we can say that he was more than a conqueror, for he conquered the great Goliath and he brought all his ammunition back with him in victory.

1 Kings 18: 31-39: "*And Elijah took twelve stones, according to the number of the tribes of the sons of Jacob, unto whom the word of the Lord came, saying, Israel shall be thy name: And with the stones he built an altar in the name of the Lord: and he made a trench about the altar, as great as would contain two measures of seed. And he put the wood in order, and cut the bullock in pieces, and laid him on the wood, and said, Fill four barrels with water, and pour it on the burnt sacrifice, and on the wood. And he said, Do it the third time. And they did it the third time. And the water ran round about the altar; and he filled the trench also with water. And it came to pass at the time of the offering of the evening sacrifice, that Elijah the prophet came near, and said, Lord God of Abraham, Isaac and of Israel, let it be known this day that thou art God in Israel, and that I am thy servant, and that I have done all these things at thy word. Hear me, O Lord, hear me, that this people may know that thou art the Lord God, and that thou hast turned their heart back again. Then the fire of the Lord fell, and consumed the burnt sacrifice, and the wood, and the stones, and the dust, and licked up the water that was in the trench.*"

Here we have Elijah gathering another group of twelve stones. This time it was for a repair job. The Lord's altar had been broken down and we read that Elijah repaired the altar of the Lord that was broken down, taking the twelve stones to make that altar anew in the name of the Lord, and we find that when the sacrifice was laid there was no fire put beneath it, because the altar fire on the Lord's altar in the Tabernacle was kindled by God. Only a heavenly fire can consume the heavenly sacrifice, and the fire had to be rekindled, the altar had to be repaired. When Elijah cried unto God the fire of the Lord fell, and it not only consumed the burnt sacrifice and the wood and the dust, but the very stones, and it licked up all the water that was in the trench. Here we have the gathering of stones, the repairing of God's altar, the rekindling of God's fire, bringing about a great revival, so that those who beforehand halted between two opinions, halted no more but cried out, 'The Lord, He is the God; the Lord, He is the God.'

In these days of apostasy we need to gather stones in this way, we need to do the repair job, we need to pray for the rekindling job, and we need to move to the enjoyment of a great revival of true religion.

Turn now to Psalm 102:13-16: *"Thou shalt arise, and have mercy upon Zion: for the time to favour her, yea the set time, is come. For thy servants take pleasure in her stones, and favour the dust thereof. So the heathen shall fear the name of the Lord, and all the kings of the earth thy glory When the Lord shall build up Zion, he shall appear in his glory."*

Here we have the theme of revival carried forward, the preciousness of the foundation stones recaptured. The very dust of those stones is precious to the true servants of the Lord. In their heart there is kindled a great hope, for they believe that the time to favour Zion is coming again, that God has a set time for reviving His people, and they believe it must be the breaking of the day when God shall build up Zion and Zion shall recover her former glories, and the heathen shall have cause to fear the name of the Lord. Happy prospects for the church of Jesus Christ in the coming days. God has not forsaken His church and never will. When He comes the church will not be a bedraggled, defeated, depressed, disappointed and dismayed church, but she will be as a bride adorned for her husband. Nothing can adorn the church but a great outpouring of the Holy Spirit and a great renewal of God's life in the hearts of His people.

Gather stones in expectancy of that great revival of true religion.

The last scripture text on the gathering of stones I wish to refer to is in Isaiah 54:11,12: *"O thou afflicted, tossed with tempest, and not comforted, behold, I will lay thy stones with fair colours, and lay thy foundations with sapphires. And I will make thy windows of agates, and thy gates of carbuncles, and all thy borders of pleasant stones. And all thy children shall be taught of the Lord; and great shall be the peace of thy children."*

Here we have God gathering stones. Here we have God building in these stones, here we have the building of the supreme temple of God. Do not be disturbed in heart, thou afflicted chiid of God. Those of you whose little ship is tossed in the tempest, do not be dismayed, for God is gathering and God is laying stones, stones of fair colours, stones of sapphires, stones of agates, stones of carbuncles and stones that are described as pleasant stones. What a glorious building it is, when God's own gathered stones are built into the foundation and fabric and finish of His church. The future of the church is as bright as the promises of God, and those promises are shining more and more unto the perfect day. And so let us all be engaged in gathering the stones together, gathering them from out of the Jordan river, gathering them to make an entrance, a doorway into the land that flows with milk and honey, gathering them to do battle with the enemies of the gospel, gathering them to be a part of that glorious work of grace and the reviving and the repairing and the refreshment of the church, and gathering them with God as our partner in the final glories of the church of the first-born ones whose names are written in heaven.

For such a time as this is surely a time to gather stones together.

A TIME TO EMBRACE AND A TIME TO REFRAIN FROM EMBRACING
ECCLESIASTES 3 V 5

A TIME TO EMBRACE

We turn first of all to the time to embrace. Our first scripture is in Genesis 29:13,14. *"And it came to pass, when Laban heard the tidings of Jacob his sister's son, that he ran to meet him, and embraced him, and kissed him, and brought him to his house. And he told Laban all these things. And Laban said to him. Surely thou art bone of my bone and flesh of my flesh. And he abode with him the space of a month."*

Here we have the embracing of those related by birth. Surely those who are related by birth should always be in the spirit of love with their relations and should be ready to make it a time to embrace. Jacob had been driven from home because of his elder brother's threat. He left his father who thought he was going to die, but didn't die until forty years later, and his mother who was in perfect health. He saw his father again but he never saw his mother again. Now he comes to his mother's brother who receives him. He not only received him, but he embraced him and kissed him and brought him into his house and marked the relationship with the words, "Surely thou art my bone and my flesh."

A time of embracing can be either a time of sincerity or a time of hypocrisy. Alas for Jacob, Laban's welcome and Laban's embrace and Laban's kiss and Laban's words of unity deteriorated into the vilest of hypocrisy, when the kiss was a kiss of betrayal, when the embrace was an act of denial and when the welcome was one which could have been fatal for Jacob.

As we go through the world there is certainly a time to embrace, a time to kiss, a time to welcome and a time to confess. Surely in such a time as this we should know such love in our hearts for those related to us, and especially those related to us in the grace of God, that we should be able to welcome them sincerely, embrace them sincerely, kiss them sincerely, and bring them into our house sincerely, and reaffirm that they are bone of our bone and flesh of our flesh. We must, however, safeguard ourselves from all hypocrisy and search our own hearts and see that we never give the insincere embrace, the insincere kiss, the insincere welcome or the insincere word of respect and love. We can be guilty of the same sin as Laban. We must discern those who would embrace us, those who would kiss us, those who would welcome us, those who would affirm their affiliation to us, whether they are sincere. To be wounded in the house of one's friends is to endure the greatest wound of all.

O for a heart that is pure! O for a love that is pure! O for an embrace that is pure!

O for a kiss that is pure! O for words of welcome that are pure!. In their purity we can delight, and in their unbreakable joy we can enter with relish.

In Genesis 33:4 we have the meeting between the estranged brothers, Jacob and Esau. "And Esau ran to meet him and embraced him and fell on his neck and kissed him and they wept."

Here we have Esau demonstrating his love to Jacob. It was a love that ran. It was a love that embraced. It was a love that fell on his neck. It was a love that kissed him and they both wept. At that point I believe Esau's love was sincere, that his embrace was sincere, that his falling on Jacob's neck was sincere, and his kiss to Jacob was sincere and that they both were sincere in their tears. But that love, that embrace, did not last. It soon corroded and decayed and the hatred at the first became a greater hatred in the end and when we read the sad story of the sons and daughters and the tribe of Esau we see that to the very end they hated Israel, they hated Jacob's inheritance and they hated Jacob's children and his children's children. The end of the story was a demonstration of a sincere embrace that through the years didn't last, a sincere kiss that didn't last, sincere tears that didn't last. We need guard against the corrosion of time. We need to guard against those things that come to turn our joys into sorrows and our sincerity into hypocrisy. The sad story of Esau and the resurgence of his desperate and terrible hatred of Jacob and all that he was and all that he possessed and all of his posterity. A time to embrace - but make sure that the embrace is going to last. Make sure that the kiss is going to last. Make sure that the friendship is going to last.

Genesis 48: 8-14: "*And Israel beheld Joseph's sons, and said, Who are these? And Joseph said unto his father, They are my sons, whom God hath given me in this place. And he said, Bring them, I pray thee, unto me, and I will bless them.*

Now the eyes of Israel were dim for age, so that he could not see. And he brought them near unto him; and he kissed them, and embraced them. And Israel said unto Joseph, I had not thought to see thy face: and, lo, God hath shewed me also thy seed. And Joseph brought them out from between his knees, and he bowed himself with his face to the earth. And Joseph took them both, Ephraim in his right hand toward Israel's left hand, and Manasseh in his left hand toward Israel's right hand, and brought them near unto him. And Israel stretched out his right hand, and laid it upon Ephraim's head, who was the younger and his left hand upon Manasseh's head, guiding his hands wittingly; for Manasseh was the first born."

Let us return to verse 10. "*Now the eyes of Israel were dim for age so that he could not see and he brought them near unto him and he kissed them and embraced them.*" Here we have the kiss that has behind it the entire life and the entire depths of love in that life. Israel, once Jacob, but now a prince with God, has his last meeting with his two grandsons, the sons of his beloved Joseph. And although his eyes were dimmed that he could not see, he was able to kiss the boys and embrace them. What a wonderful scene. The old man Israel, ready to pass over another Jordan and to the throne where his father Abraham and his father Isaac worship God. And he said to Joseph, "I thought I would never see thy face again but God in his greatness, goodness and graciousness has brought me to see your seed." And in the compassion of a heart that was breaking and with thankfulness to God for His unfailing goodness, he embraced his grandsons and kissed them. What an embrace, the embrace of the prince! What a kiss, the kiss of strength! Oh to embrace our spiritual fruit as Jacob here embraces his natural fruit. Oh to kiss our spiritual children as Jacob kissed and embraced his natural children.

There is something that binds the spiritual father to the spiritual child. There is something that causes the spiritual father to kiss his spiritual child. It is a love unknown naturally but a love that is in spirit and in truth for it is because Christ loved us that this depth of love is manifested in our hearts.

II Kings 4:16,17: *"And he said (i.e. Elisha), About this season, according to the time of life, thou shalt embrace a son. And she said, Nay, my lord, thou man of God, do not lie unto thine handmaid. And the woman conceived, and bear a son at that season that Elisha had said unto her, according to the time of life."*

Here is the prospect of a sweet embrace. This dear woman had no son. Every woman of Israel wanted to have as son for perchance her son would be the promised Messiah. It was looked upon in Israel as a judgment if a woman begat no sons. All through the historical scriptures this is made perfectly clear. The longing desire for a woman in Israel to be the mother of a son, who perhaps would be the long awaited Messiah, the Saviour of mankind.

This woman had given up all hope. This woman had given up all thought. This woman had given up all desire. She thought that she would go to the grave in barrenness. Then through her goodness to Elisha there came a promise. And he said, *"according to the time of life, thou shalt embrace a son"*. Those words had a tremendous effect upon that woman. All the hopes that had been dead were suddenly resurrected. All the desires that had fled away now came back with fury. All the wonder of being a mother was resurrected within her heart and mind and life.

And she said, *"Nay, my lord ... do not lie unto thine handmaid."* What was she saying? She was saying, "You could not touch a more tender spot, you could not cause more dismay and more hopelessness and more darkness and despair than to try and relight a hope that can never be ignited. But the despair was not to be. This was not the lie but the truth and the woman did conceive and bore a son as the prophet had told her.

The Bible is filled with promises, promises of our embracing the very things we thought were lost and gone forever; promises of a light that still keeps burning and shines more and more unto the perfect day; promises that now are not but will be; promises that seem impossible, but nothing is impossible with our God; promises that we think can never be fulfilled, but will be fulfilled above all that we can ask or think. I wonder how that woman felt as she first embraced her little baby son. How tenderly she must have touched his baby hands. With what compassion she must have watched his every look and responded to his every cry. I wonder how deeply her heart was touched that day in love to her God who had given her this hope that she thought could never be hers. At a time like this there is a time to embrace, a future prospect.

Surely we should all be ready to exercise faith and embrace the prospect still to come.

A TIME TO REFRAIN FROM EMBRACING

Proverbs 5:15-21: *"Drink waters out of thine own cistern, and running waters out of thine own well. Let thy fountains be dispersed abroad, and rivers of waters in the streets. Let them be only thine own, and not strangers' with thee. Let thy fountain be blessed: and rejoice with the wife of thy youth. Let her be as the loving hind and pleasant roe: let her breasts satisfy thee at all times; and be thou ravished always with her love.* ***And why wilt thou, my son, be ravished with a strange woman, and embrace the bosom of a stranger?*** *For the ways of man are before the eyes of the Lord, and he pondereth all his goings."*

In this day of immorality, in this day of iniquity, in this day of loose living and uncleanness and impurity, this question needs to be asked. In such a time as this there can be no place for embracing the bosom of a stranger. The Bible tells us here, *"Drink waters out of thine own cistern, and running waters out of thine own well. "* It says concerning the wife of our youth, *"Let her be as the loving hind and pleasant roe: let her breasts satisfy thee at all times; and be thou ravished always with her love. "* The tragedy of today is that this day has left the Divine standard. It has lost the thrill and satisfaction of pure love within the marriage bond. It has gone into a country that is banned. It has climbed over a barrier that should not have been climbed over. It has tried to find real joy in sin and it finds it not, and burning with lust it proceeds on to more and more uncleanness, on to more and more perversion and on to more and more iniquity.

There are some things that we must not and cannot, and if we walk with God, will not embrace. How sad it is that the sweetest and dearest gift to mankind physically, the grace of life is abused the way it is today. There is no happiness. There is no satisfaction. There is no rest at all in the land that people seek outside the will of God. Bypath Meadow is the way to utter destruction. The prohibited country is a way to disaster and the place that God has said we should not go, but if we do go that is the sure way to disappointment, despair, distress, disaster, death and damnation.

In such a time as this let us obey God rather than men. Let us crucify our affections and lusts. Let us walk the path of purity asking for the old paths, questioning for the old ways, that we may walk therein. And in those ways we will find the ways of pleasantness and in those paths we will find the paths of peace.

Joel 2:15-17 *"Blow the trumpet in Zion, sanctify a fast, call a solemn assembly: Gather the people, sanctify the congregation, assemble the elders, gather the children, and those that suck the breasts: let the bridegroom go forth of his chamber, and the bride out of her closet."*

Here we have a commandment that there is a time to refrain from embracing. The bridegroom must go forth from his chamber and the bride must go forth out of her closet. The priests, the ministers of God, must leave their families and weep between the porch and the altar. For such a time as this, yes this time when the church is at sixes and sevens, this time when the whole earth has gone a-whoring after peace; this time when evil prevails, and spiritual darkness and destitution have flooded in upon this world, this is a time to refrain from human embracing and to turn to God and embrace His promises, embrace His will, embrace His purpose, and cry out for the vindicaton of God. For are not the heathen of the world saying to the believer today "Where is thy God?" Let us remember that the Lord will be jealous for His land and He shall pity His people.

So when we refuse to embrace but turn rather to embrace God, then God will richly reward us.

In such a time as this there is need for us to disengage ourselves from embracing. It is surely a time when we must refrain from such embracing.

A TIME TO GET AND A TIME TO LOSE

ECCLESIASTES 3 V 6

A TIME TO GET

A time to get. The word there is a time to buy or acquire. Genesis 42:2 *"And he"* (that is Jacob) *"said, Behold, I have heard that there is corn in Egypt: get you down thither, and buy for us from thence; that we may live, and not die."* Verse 7 *"And Joseph saw his brethren, and he knew them, but made himself strange unto them, and spake roughly unto them; and he said unto them, Whence come ye? And they said, From the land of Canaan to buy food."*

A further great famine had fallen in Canaan. If they could not get food they would die. They had heard that there was corn in Egypt. It was a time to get, a time to buy, a time to acquire. So Jacob ordered them down into Egypt to acquire, to buy, to get the bread they needed.

Little did they think that the famine was the most bountiful thing that ever came to Canaan, for without that famine Joseph's brethren would never have found Joseph, and Joseph would never have found his brethren.

There is a time in the affairs of this life when circumstances are against us and we think there is no benefit for us from what is happening. This is the very time to get, to buy and to acquire as Joseph's brethren found.

Ruth 4:5 *"Then said Boaz, What day thou buyest the field of the hand of Naomi, thou must buy it also of Ruth the Moabitess, the wife of the dead, to raise up the name of the dead upon his inheritance."*

Here we have another verse concerning the getting and the buying. This time it is a beautiful type of our Lord Jesus Christ who is the Great Kinsman. When He buys and acquires and gets, it is for all eternity. Surely this is the day, in such a time as this, when we should be pressing the claims of the Greater Boaz, the Greater Kinsman Redeemer upon sinners lost and ruined and without an inheritance. In Christ, the One Who bought for them redemption, they can get the greatest getting that is known in time and the greatest getting that is known in eternity, the gift of God's well Beloved Son.

Thanks be unto God for His unspeakable gift.

II Samuel 24:20-25 *"And Araunah looked, and saw the king and his servants coming on toward him: and Araunah went out, and bowed himself before the king on his face upon the ground. And Araunah said, Wherefore is my lord the king come to his servant? And David said, To buy the threshingfloor of thee, to build an altar unto the Lord, that the plague may be stayed from the people. And Araunah said unto David, Let my lord the king take and offer up what seemeth good unto him: behold, here be oxen for burnt sacrifice, and threshing instruments and other instruments of the oxen for wood. All these things did Araunah, as a king, give unto the king. And Araunah said unto the king, The Lord thy God accept thee. And the king said unto Araunah, Nay; but I will surely buy it of thee at a price: neither will I offer burnt offerings unto the Lord my God of that which doth cost me nothing. So David bought the threshingfloor and the oxen for fifty shekels of silver. And David built there an altar unto the Lord, and offered burnt offerings and peace offerings. So the Lord was intreated for the land, and the plague was stayed from Israel."*

Here we have the story of the terrible catastrophe that had fallen upon the kingdom of David because of his sin. A pestilence was sweeping the country. The angel with the sword was about to strike Jerusalem, but God gave directions to David how the sword could be deviated from drinking the blood of the people to drinking the blood of the sacrifice.

We have the story of David coming to buy the threshingfloor. There is a time to buy, to acquire, to get. You will notice that although David was offered the threshingfloor for nothing, he did not seek a way that would cost him nothing. He said unto the owner Araunah *"Nay; but I will surely buy it of thee at a price: neither will I offer burnt offerings unto the Lord my God of that which doth cost me nothing. So David bought the threshingfloor and the oxen for fifty shekels of silver."*

Notice there was a price to be paid, and the price could only be in that which typifies redemption money, the silver. Oh thank God today that there was One Who paid the full price for us on the Cross, the Greater David. He deflected the sword from our hearts to His heart and we, through the blood of His redemption, are bought with a great price. We ought therefore in such a time as this to glorify God in our bodies and our spirits which are the Lord's.

Isaiah 55:1 *"Ho, every one that thirsteth, come ye to the waters, and he that hath no money: come ye, buy, and eat; yea, come, buy wine and milk without money and without price."*

Here is a getting, here an acquiring that does not regard a human payment. This, of course, is grace at work. Grace not only supplies the ransom but supplies the coin to pay for the ransom. So we can come, our ears ringing with the Gospel invitation, and we can buy bread, we can buy wine and milk, without money and without price.

Today in such a time as this we can cry out "Come ye, come ye to the waters. Come ye that have no money, come, buy wine and milk." There is no price to be paid. If it was at a price you could never pay it, for the grace of God has paid the price and we are saved from going down to the pit of hell because Christ has paid the ransom with His precious, precious blood.

A TIME TO LOSE

Genesis 31:25-28 *"Then Laban overtook Jacob. Now Jacob had pitched his tent in the mount: and Laban with his brethren pitched in the mount of Gilead. And Laban said to Jacob, What hast thou done, that thou hast stolen away unawares to me, and carried away my daughters, as captives taken with the sword? Wherefore didst thou flee away secretly, and steal away from me; and didst not tell me, that I might have sent thee away with mirth, and with songs, with tabret, and with harp? And hast not suffered me to kiss my sons and my daughters? thou hast now done foolishly in so doing. It is in the power of my hand to do you hurt: but the God of your father spake unto me yesternight, saying, Take thou heed that thou speak not to Jacob either good or bad."*

Here Laban is seeking to recover that which is lost. He has lost his daughters, his grandchildren, his faithful servant and slave, Jacob. He has lost all that Jacob had gained in his wages, and more. Now he tries to recover what he has lost. But there is a time to lose. This was the losing time for Laban.

He intended to do Jacob ill. He probably intended to slay him, recover his daughters and bring his children back under his control. He decided to recover all that he had given to Jacob by the wages that Jacob rightly earned. God stopped him and God showed him, although it was in the power of his hand to do Jacob hurt, God said, "Take heed that thou speak not to Jacob either good or bad." It was the time for this man to lose.

There is a time to lose. When God sets up a barrier we should not cross it. When God directs us we should heed His direction. When God warns us we should open our hearts in obedience to obey that warning.

At such a time as this there is the fact and the truth of losing.

Matthew 10:39, the Lord Jesus Christ is the speaker, *"He that findeth his life shall lose it: and he that loseth his life for my sake shall find it."*

It is the time to lose. To lose the old life, the life of sin, the life of wickedness, the life of Christ-rejection, the life of worldliness, the life of pleasure, the life that is only for time, and to gain that life which is forever. He that loseth his life shall for Christ's sake find it and he that findeth his life and holds on to it shall lose it forever.

This is the truth of the Gospel. Be not satisfied with the temp-oral. Lose it and you will then be satisfied with the eternal embracing. Hold on to it, acquire it, buy it and keep it.

This is surely the time for the right type of losing.

The words of the Lord Jesus Christ again. Matthew 16:24-26 *"Then said Jesus unto his disciples, If any man will come after me, let him deny himself, and take up his cross, and follow me. For whosoever will save his life shall lose it; and whosoever will lose his life for my sake shall find it. For what is a man profited, if he shall gain the whole world, and lose his own soul? or what shall a man give in exchange for his soul?"*

Are you going to hold on to an unprofitless world? If you do, you might gain it all but you will lose your own soul. Are you going to save your life? Then you must lose it. Whosoever will lose his life for Christ's sake shall really find it. It is time, in such a time as this to be a loser according to this teaching of our Lord and Saviour Jesus Christ.

Isaiah 47: 9 *"But these two things shall come to thee in a moment in one day, the loss of children, and widowhood: they shall come upon thee in their perfection for the multitude of thy sorceries, and for the great abundance of thine enchantments."*

Here is a loss which God will inflict in judgment upon Babylon. The whole Babylonian system of Rome will rock and perish forever. Oh there is a losing day coming for the false faiths and false religions of this world. It will be their time to lose and to lose for evermore. Therefore, "Come out of her my people and receive not of her plagues," is the command of the Saviour.

In such a time as this never ever forget that there is a time to lose.

A TIME TO KEEP AND A TIME TO CAST AWAY
ECCLESIASTES 3 V 6

A TIME TO KEEP

I Samuel 16:11 *"And Samuel said unto Jesse, Are here all thy children? And he said, There remaineth yet the youngest, and, behold, he keepeth the sheep."*

For David it was a time to keep the sheep. The lion and the bear still roamed the hills of Bethlehem. The sheep were in danger and for David it was a time to keep the sheep.

Most important things were happening in Bethlehem but until David was summoned by his father and his master he abode by the stock. He kept the sheep.

In such a time as this there is a time to keep.

Proverbs 7:1-2 *"My son, keep my words, and lay up my commandments with thee. Keep my commandments, and live; and my law as the apple of thine eye."*

There is something that must always be kept. That something is the Word of the Living God, the commandments of the Holy Scripture.

This is the day of breaking the commandments. This is the day of not keeping and guarding the commandments. This is the day when the law is not as the apple of our eyes to us.

Here comes the great thunder of Divine instruction to the deaf ears of a sinful world, calling to His own people, those who are of the family of God, "My son, keep my words and lay up my commandments with thee." For us all in such a time as this it is our duty to know it is a time to keep, a time to keep the law and the commandments of our God.

In Luke's Gospel chapter 8 verse 15 the Lord Jesus Christ tells us of the seed which fell on good ground, *"But that on the good ground are they, which in an honest and good heart, having heard the word, keep it, and bring forth fruit with patience."*

Here we have Christ's comment on the good seed that brings forth good fruit, some thirty, some sixty and some a hundredfold. Who are they? They are those with a good heart who having heard the Word, keep it. Keeping the Word of God, guarding the Word of God, preserving the Word of God, obeying the Word of God, being led by the Word of God, being captivated by the Word of God, being driven by the Word of the Living God.

In such a time as this it is the time to keep the good seed in the Lord's harvest field.

Let us listen to the commandment of God in II Timothy 1:14 *"That good thing which was committed unto thee keep by the Holy Ghost which dwelleth in us."*

We need the power of the Holy Ghost to keep and to ever know that this is the hour of keeping by the Holy Ghost that good and perfect Word of God.

A TIME TO CAST AWAY

In Judges 15 verses 14-19 we have an incident recorded in the life of the mighty Samson. *"And when he came unto Le-hi, the Philistines shouted against him; and the Spirit of the Lord came mightily upon him, and the cords that were upon his arms became as flax that was burnt with fire, and his bands loosed from off his hands. And he found a new jaw-bone of an ass, and put forth his hand, and took it, and slew a thousand men therewith. And Samson said, With the jawbone of an ass, heaps upon heaps, with the jaw of an ass have I slain a thousand men. And it came to pass, when he had made an end of speaking, that he cast away the jawbone out of his hand and called that place Ramathlehi. And he was sore athirst and called on the Lord, and said, Thou hast given this great deliverance into the hand of thy servant: and now shall I die for thirst, and fall into the hand of the uncircumcised? But God clave an hollow place that was in the jaw, and there came water thereout; and when he had drunk, his spirit came again, and he revived: wherefore he called the name thereof Enhakkore, which is in Le-hi unto this day."*

Here we have an episode of casting away. When the great battle was over, when Samson had slain one thousand of the uncircumcised Philistines, he thought the job was concluded and to him it was a time to cast away. But he cast away the jawbone too speedily, and he became thirsty and weak unto death.

The jawbone that brought death to the enemies of God was to be the instrument that brought life to Samson. So back to the jawbone he had to go, and God clave within the jaw a place that became a spring of living water. When he had drunk the water his spirit came again and he revived. He called the place thereof Enhakkore which is in Le-hi unto this day.

Thank God we have a Bible, a Bible which can completely rout the enemy, but we have a Bible which becomes not only death to the enemy but life to us.

There is a time to cast out in sowing the Word of God to compel His enemies to surrender. There is a time not to cast away the Book for we will need its healing and life-giving power.

II Kings 7:12-17 *"And the King arose in the night, and said unto his servants, I will now shew you what the Syrians have done to us. They know that we be hungry; therefore are they gone out of the camp to hide themselves in the field, saying, When they come out of the city, we shall catch them alive, and get into the city. And one of his servants answered and said, Let some take, I pray thee, five of the horses that remain, which are left in the city, (behold, they are as all the multitude of Israel that are left in it: behold, I say, they are even as all the multitude of the Israelites that are consumed:) and let us send and see. They took therefore two chariot horses; and the king sent after the host of the Syrians, saying, Go and see. And they went after them unto Jordan: and, lo, all the way was full of garments and vessels, which the Syrians had cast away in their haste. And the messengers returned, and told the king. And the people went out, and spoiled the tents of the Syrians. So a measure of fine flour was sold for a shekel, and two measures of barley for a shekel, according to the word of the Lord."*

Note especially verse 15 *"And they went after them unto Jordan: and, lo, all the way was full of garments and vessels, which the Syrians had cast away in their haste."* The Syrians thought they were going to destroy the city. They thought that the city would be finally destroyed and that they would be the conquerors. It was not to be. God had ordered something different for the city of Samaria.

We see here the intervention of Almighty God, so much so that the enemy in their flight had to cast away every possession in order to escape what they thought was impending disaster.

The Syrians' defeat was complete when they cast away their possessions. For them it was a time to cast away because their very possessions, which they loved and which seemed to be an enrichment, turned out, in their muddled brains, to be a great and terrible opposition to the possibility of their making their escape.

Isaiah 31:6-7 *"Turn ye unto him from whom the children of Israel have deeply revolted. For in that day every man shall cast away his idols of silver, and his idols of gold, which your own hands have made unto you for a sin."*

The time comes when religious error must be cast away and religious idolatry must be forsaken; when the idols must be broken and when the baubles of Babylon must be forever destroyed. Every man shall cast away his idols of silver for there is no redemption there and his idols of gold, for there is no enrichment there. They will cast them away with their very own hands and not assisted by the hands of others.

This is surely the time idolater, to cast away your idols. For such a time as this is a time to eschew all idolatry. Flee youthful lusts and have done with idolatries of the heart.

Hosea 9:17 *"My God will cast them away, because they did not hearken unto him: and they shall be wanderers among the nations."*

Here we have God casting away those who cast not away their idols; God forsaking those who will not forsake their idols; God saying goodbye to those who will not say goodbye to their apostasy. What a terrible thing when it is God's time to cast men and their precious souls away from hope, away from peace, away from pardon and away from forgiveness. Cast away, cast out into outer darkness, and there shall be weeping and wailing and gnashing of teeth.

In such a time as this the judgments of God are upon the earth and God is casting away people, people with hardened hearts and disobedient spirits and sinful lives and they become wanderers, like Cain, upon the face of the earth.

Ecclesiastes 11:1 *"Cast thy bread upon the waters: for thou shalt find it after many days. Give a portion to seven, and also to eight; for thou knowest not what evil shall be upon the earth."*

Many years ago a man tied, fettered and chained with sin came to see me. His plight was one of absolute and abject misery. He had no power. He could not resist the evil nor could he hold on to the good. A powerless sinner, guilty and undone. No one wanted to know him or know about him.

We brought him to our home. We dressed him and fed him and kept him and slowly the grace of God worked in his heart. He then left us and went away.

Over thirty years later, we received a letter. It was a letter of deep thanksgiving to God and expressing gratitude to us, recording his past, recording his needs and recording his despair but recording also the work of God in his heart. Bread cast upon the waters was returning to us after many days.

That man went to London. He came from darkness to light by the Word of God which we had sown in his heart. He became a missionary to the down and outs in the great city of London. He made a good marriage with a Christian girl and they had two sons of whom they are justly proud.

His older son, he told me, had just graduated from university and his younger son was about to enter university. He said, "I think of you and I thank God for the words you spoke, for the goodness of your wife in receiving me and keeping me." Yes, when bread is cast upon the waters it does most certainly return. I could record, in my over fifty years of ministry, the glorious days of returning bread, when the bread returns fresher than in the day it was baked or sent forth or cast forth; when the bread is fresher than when it first went out on its errand; when the bread is not mildewed or moulded but is in pristine condition, as fresh as it came from the mouth of God.

Yes, cast your bread upon the waters, for there is a time to cast away and that time is the time of prospect and the time of opportunity.

A TIME TO REND AND A TIME TO SEW
ECCLESIASTES 3 V 7

A TIME TO REND

In I Samuel 15 :20, Saul has returned from fighting the Amalekites but in abject failure because he did not utterly destroy them, as he was commanded by the Lord. Verse 20-29: *"And Saul said unto Samuel, Yea, I have obeyed the voice of the Lord, and have gone the way which the Lord sent me, and have brought Agag the king of Amakek, and have utterly destroyed the Amalekites. But the people took of the spoil, sheep and oxen, the chief of the things which should have been utterly destroyed, to sacrifice unto the Lord thy God in Gilgal. And Samuel said, Hath the Lord as great delight in burnt offerings and sacrifices, as in obeying the voice of the Lord? Behold, to obey is better than sacrifice, and to hearken than the fat of rams. For rebellion is as the sin of witchcraft, and stubbornness is as iniquity and idolatry. Because thou hast rejected the word of the Lord, he hath also rejected thee from being king. And Saul said unto Samuel, I have sinned: for I have transgressed the commandment of the Lord, and thy words: because I feared the people, and obeyed their voice. Now therefore, I pray thee, pardon my sin, and turn again with me, that I may worship the Lord. And Samuel said unto Saul, I will not return with thee: for thou hast rejected the word of the Lord, and the Lord hath rejected thee from being king over Israel. And as Samuel turned about to go away, he laid hold upon the skirt of his mantle, and it rent. And Samuel said unto him, The Lord hath rent the kingdom of Israel from thee this day, and hath given it to a neighbour of thine, that is better than thou. And also the Strength of Israel will not lie nor repent: for he is not a man, that he should repent."*

There are some verses here which we need to take knowledge of, especially verse 27: *"And as Samuel turned about to go away, he laid hold upon the skirt of his mantle, and it rent. And Samuel said unto him, The Lord hath rent the kingdom of Israel from thee this day, and hath given it to a neighbour of thine, that is better than thou."*

Here we have the rending of justice and a rending in the pathway of the separation of the chaff from the wheat and the pure from the filthy, and there was a rending that was complete and could not be gone back on. For Samuel said, "the Strength of Israel will not lie nor repent: for he is not a man, that he should repent."

The final stroke of judgment on Saul was at the time to rend, when the garment of Samuel was torn and when the kingdom was torn from the first king of Israel, king Saul. The pathway of separation was the pathway where there was a complete rending from the two parties in the dispute, the true prophet of God and the king who had apostatized.

In I Kings 11: 9-13 we have another passage of Scripture which illustrates a time to rend. It is an incident in the life of the great King Solomon. Solomon has done wrong and God said, in verse 11, *"I will surely rend the kingdom from thee, and will give it to thy servant."*

As we read on in that chapter we have the prophet Ahijah the Shilonite and he said to Jeroboam, having torn a new garment in twelve pieces, verse 31, *"Take thee ten pieces: for thus saith the Lord, the God of Israel, Behold, I will rend the kingdom out of the hand of Solomon, and will give ten tribes to thee."*

When we turn over to the fourteenth chapter of the same book we read the judgment upon the very same man who got the ten pieces, Jeroboam, and the same prophet said in chapter 7 *"Go tell Jeroboam, Thus saith the Lord God of Israel, Forasmuch as I exalted thee from among the people, and made thee prince over my people Israel, and rent the kingdom away from the house of David, and gave it to thee: and yet thou hast not been as my servant David, who kept my commandments, and who followed me with all his heart, to do that only which was right in mine eyes."*

So here was judgment upon Saul, judgment upon Solomon and judgment upon Jeroboam. The time to rend had come.

Over in the book of Joel, one of the minor prophets, in chapter 2 and verse 12 we read, *"Therefore also now, saith the Lord, turn ye even to me with all your heart, and with fasting, and with weeping, and with mourning; and rend your heart and not your garments, and turn unto the Lord your God; for he is gracious, and merciful, slow to anger, and of great kindness, and repenteth him of the evil. Who knoweth if he will return and repent and leave a blessing behind him; even a meat offering and a drink offering unto the Lord your God."*

Here, instead of a time of judgment is a time leading from judgment to reviving and pardoning and blessing. Oh that today we might rend these cold, hard hearts of ours. Oh that today God might tear away everything that savours of darkness and worldliness and sin and that our hearts, rent and purified, might become the dwelling place of the mighty spirit of God so that we can be used in this dark day as beacons of light shining forth in the darkness of the world.

Last of all, could I draw your attention to the rending that did not take place, although it was first designed and desired to take place.

John 19:23 *"Then the soldiers, when they had crucified Jesus, took his garments, and made four parts, to every soldier a part; and also his coat: now the coat was without seam, woven from the top throughout. They said therefore among themselves, Let us not rend it, but cast lots for it, whose it shall be: that the scripture might be fulfilled, which saith, They parted my raiment among them, and for my vesture they did cast lots. These things therefore the soldiers did."*

Thank God the blessed seamless robe of Christ's righteousness typified in this outer garment, the coat, can never be rent or torn. It stands unageing and unbreakable, offered by grace to the sinner who will put his trust in Christ alone for salvation.

Jesus, Thy blood and righteousness
My beauty are, my glorious dress;
Mid'st flaming worlds, in these arrayed,
With joy shall I lift up my head.

Bold shall I stand in that great day,
For who aught to my charge shall lay?
Fully absolved through Thee I am,
From sin and fear, from guilt and shame.

A TIME TO SEW

"Sow" means to join together, to adjust. We have been reading about the rending in its reference to the kingdoms and judgment. Now we are thinking of the sewing and we are thinking of the references to joining together and adjusting.

Over in the great book of Ezekiel chapter 37:15 *"The word of the Lord came again unto me, saying, Moreover, thou son of man, take thee one stick, and write upon it. For Judah, and for the children of Israel his companions; then take another stick, and write upon it, For Joseph, the stick of Ephraim, and for all the house of Israel his companions; And join them one to another into one stick; and they shall become one in thine hand."* Verse 23 *"Neither shall they defile themselves any more with their idols, nor with their detestable things, nor with any of their transgressions: but I will save them out of all their dwelling places, wherein they have sinned, and will cleanse them: so that they shall be my people, and I will be their God. And David my servant shall be king over them; and they all shall have one shepherd: they shall also walk in my judgments, and observe my statutes, and do them."*

Here we have the final uniting of the two nations. We have unity at last. In such a time as this we should be looking for that unity of the Spirit in the bond of peace.

Oh for a sewing time! Oh for a joining time! Oh for a uniting time!

A TIME TO KEEP SILENCE
AND A TIME TO SPEAK
ECCLESIASTES 3 V 7

A TIME TO KEEP SILENT

Leviticus 10:3 *"Then Moses said unto Aaron, This is it that the Lord spake, saying, I will be sanctified in them that come nigh me, and before all the people I will be glorified. And Aaron held his peace."*

A time to be silent.

Yes, and well may Aaron be silent. His two sons, Nadab and Abihu, had taken to the drink and then they had taken to offering strange fire before the Lord, which brought about swift and terrible judgment. In such a time as this there will be judgment upon drunken priests and their false sacrifice and their offering of strange fire.

Psalm 32:1-4 *"Blessed is he whose transgression is forgiven, whose sin is covered. Blessed is the man unto whom the Lord imputeth not iniquity, and in whose spirit there is no guile. When I kept silence, my bones waxed old through my roaring all the day long. For day and night thy hand was heavy upon me: my moisture is turned into the drought of summer."*

Here is a silence which must be broken, a silence which must lead to confession. There is a time for silence, a time for the sinner, (like David in this instance), to hang his head, to refuse to move his lips, stunned at his own self-indulgence, folly, sin, weakness and wickedness. Beyond the silence, there is a song; beyond the quietness the joy, for blessed is the man to whom the Lord imputeth not iniquity and in whose spirit there is no guile. In such a time as this there is a time of silence but there is also a time of song.

A TIME TO SPEAK

In the second book of the Bible, the book of Exodus 7:2, we read these words, *"Thou shalt speak all that I command thee: and Aaron thy brother shall speak unto Pharaoh, that he send the children of Israel out of his land."*

The time had come, in this passage of Scripture, when the voice of God's commandment must be heard in the imperial palace of Egypt and by the mighty king Pharaoh.

Moses complained that he was not a speaker and God said, "Who has made man's mouth?" When he insisted, God said, "There is Aaron, your brother, he is known as a very eloquent speaker. He will be your mouthpiece. I will speak to you, you will convey to him My word and he will convey and proclaim that word to Pharaoh."

So Aaron became the spokesman of God, for the time was a time to speak.

God has never left himself without a spokesman and God will raise up spokesmen for Himself who will deliver faithfully the Word of the living God. We should pray today for real prophet-like preachers who shall take their place on the walls of Zion and shall proclaim the truth of the Gospel in all its fulness and in all its integrity.

Nathan the prophet was called upon to speak to David when David had sinned. It was a time to speak and Nathan said "Thou art the man." But Nathan also delivered a message to David. In II Samuel 7:12 -17 it is recorded, *"And when thy days be fulfilled, and thou shalt sleep with thy fathers, I will set up thy seed after thee, which shall proceed out of thy bowels, and I will establish his kingdom. He shall build an house for my name, and I will stablish the throne of his kingdom for ever. I will be his father, and he shall be my son. If he commit iniquity, I will chasten him with the rod of men, and with the stripes of the children of men: But my mercy shall not depart away from him, as I took it from Saul, whom I put away before thee. And thine house and thy kingdom shall be established for ever before thee: thy throne shall be established for ever. According to all these words, and according to all this vision, so did Nathan speak unto David."*

Notice how Nathan was ordered. *"According to all these words and according to all this vision so did Nathan speak unto David."* The true servant of God speaks the whole counsel of God. He withholds nothing, he diminishes nothing, he adds nothing, it is the Word of God. "Oh earth, earth, earth," cried George Whitefield, "hear the Word of the Lord."

Ezekiel 2: 6-8 *"And thou, son of man, be not afraid of them, neither be afraid of their words, though briers and thorns be with thee, and thou dost dwell among scorpions: be not afraid of their words, nor be dismayed at their looks, though they be a rebellious house. And thou shalt speak my words unto them, whether they will hear, or whether they will forbear: for they are most rebellious. But thou, son of man, hear what I say unto thee; Be not thou rebellious like that rebellious house: open thy mouth, and eat that I give thee."*

No matter what the opposition is, when the time is come the speech must be made.

Martin Luther said, "Should a certain part of the walls of Zion be attached it is that part of the wall must be defended. It is no use shoring up or defending a wall not under attack. You must defend the wall that is being attacked."

When the Word of God is directed against those who seek to demolish the building of God then the attack of the Word must be upon them. As Luther said, he who defends the unattacked wall is not the friend of truth. He is the true friend of truth and the true soldier of Christ who goes to the place where the enemy waits to attack the wall and there he stands fearlessly to defend that which is God's.

Yes, there is a time to speak, and in such a day as this there is a time to speak. Let us speak then for the Lord, faithfully telling to men the true Word of the living God.

A TIME TO LOVE AND A TIME TO HATE
ECCLESIASTES 3 V 8

A TIME TO LOVE

In Jeremiah 2:2 we read these words of the great prophet, *"Go and cry in the ears of Jersualem, saying, Thus saith the Lord; I remember thee, the kindness of thy youth, the love of thine espousals, when thou wentest after me in the wilderness, in the land that was not sown."*

Here we have the time to love and what a time is that! The time when the glory of God broke upon our darkened soul, the time when we came out of the night of our sin to the dawning of our salvation, the time when God gave to us a vision of Mount Calvary; a time when the shut eyes became open eyes and the sightless eyes became seeing eyes. We saw One who before was without any form or beauty but now to us He was the most wonderful Person in the world. There was a beauty about His countenance, a beauty about His sacrifice and what a wonderful beauty about His precious blood, flowing for our redemption.

We looked and as Spurgeon said, "looked away our eyes with looking." We looked to Him and He looked to us and we were begotten of the Lord in a second birth and partook of a love which cannot be described and whose dimensions defy all measurements of man.

Oh the love that drew salvation's plan,
O the grace that brought it down to man,
O the mighty gulf that God did span,
At Calvary.

Over in the Word of God we read in Ezekiel 16:8-14 these precious words, *"Now when I passed by thee, and looked upon thee, behold, thy time was the time of love; and I spread my skirt over thee, and covered thy nakedness; yea, I sware unto thee, and entered into a covenant with thee, saith the Lord God, and thou becamest mine. Then washed I thee with water; yea, I throughly washed away thy blood from thee, and I anointed thee with oil. I clothed thee also with embroidered work, and shod thee with badgers' skin, and I girded thee about with fine linen, and I covered thee with silk. I decked thee also with ornaments, and I put bracelets upon thy hands, and a chain on thy neck. And I put a jewel on thy forehead, and earrings in thine ears, and a beautiful crown upon thine head. Thus wast thou decked with gold and silver; and thy raiment was of fine linen, and silk, and broidered work; thou didst eat fine flour, and honey, and oil: and thou wast exceeding beautiful, and thou didst prosper into a kingdom. And thy renown went forth among the heathen for thy beauty: for it was perfect through my comeliness, which I had put upon thee, saith the Lord God."*

Notice how the Lord said it was the time of love. Oh how blessed the soul that has been brought to the love time of our Lord Jesus Christ.

How wonderful the experience to be able to say from the depths of our heart "I love him because, because, because, He first loved me."

Surely in such a time as this it is the time to proclaim the simple gospel message that "God so loved the world that He gave His only begotten Son that whosoever believeth in Him should not perish but have everlasting life."

A TIME TO HATE

Turn over in the Bible to II Samuel 13:15 *"Then Amnon hated her exceedingly; so that the hatred wherewith he hated her was greater than the love wherewith he had loved her. And Amnon said unto her, Arise, be gone."*

The thirteenth chapter of II Samuel records the terrible tragedy of the prince Ammon and of his evil, lustful intent against his own half-sister. Oh the tragedy of sin! Oh the terror of sin! and O the triumph of sin!

And for him there came a time to hate. It was the result of his wickedness. It was brought forth from the womb of lust and it was born to be cradled in wickedness and became a time to hate.

Such a hate is a hellish wickedness. But there is a hatred which is born because truth is loved, because purity is cherished and because righteousness is uplifted and defended.

In Amos 5:15 we are commanded to *"Hate the evil, and love the good."*

In Psalm 97:10 we are told that those that love God hate evil. So our hatred of evil comes from our love of God, and the measure of our hatred of evil will be the measure of our love for God.

In Proverbs 6:16 we read of the things that God hates *"These six things doth the Lord hate: yea, seven are an abomination unto him: A proud look, a lying tongue, and hands that shed innocent blood, An heart that deviseth wicked imaginations, feet that be swift in running to mischief, A false witness that speaketh lies, and he that soweth discord among brethren."*

These things that the Lord hates we have to hate because we love Him and all His ways.

In Psalm 101:3 the Psalmist said, *"I will set no wicked thing before mine eyes: I hate the work of them that turn aside; it shall not cleave to me."* I hate the work of them that turn aside.

In Psalm 119:104 David said, *"Through my precepts I get understanding: therefore I hate every false way."* He repeats that again in 128th verse of the same Psalm. He says *"Therefore I esteem all thy precepts concerning all things to be right and I hate every false way."* In verse 113 of the same Psalm he says *"I hate vain thoughts: but thy law do I love."* In verse 163 of the same Psalm he says *"I hate and abhor lying: but thy law do I love."*

In Psalm 139:21-22 he says *"Do not I hate them, O Lord, that hate thee? and am not I grieved with those that rise up against thee. I hate them with perfect hatred: I count them mine enemies."*

So there is a time to hate and each one of us should hate the things that God hates and love the things that God loves. God's children should be great lovers and they should be great haters as well.

In such a time as this there is a time to love and there is a time to hate.

A TIME OF WAR AND A TIME OF PEACE
ECCLESIASTES 3 V 8

A TIME OF WAR

Exodus 17:15-16 *"And Moses built an altar, and called the name of it Jehovah nissi: For he said, Because the Lord hath sworn that the Lord will have war with Amalek from generation to generation."*

Here we have the Lord's righteous war against the would-be destroyer and annihilator of God's chosen people. Amalek is a type of Satan and God's war against Satan will continue until Satan is cast into the lake of fire.

There is a righteous war, the war of God against Satan, the war of God's truth against the devil's lie, the war of God's pardon against the counterfeit pardons of hell, the war of God's Christ against the antichrist, the war of righteousness against unrighteousness, and the war of heaven against hell.

That war has been raging since the time of the satanic rebellion among the angels of God in heaven. The apostasy of Lucifer, the cherub, and his casting down by God from his high place. That war will continue, and mankind will be caught up in the sweep of that war until this world comes to an end and time is no more, and eternity has come and a new heaven and a new earth have been created in which there shall dwell everlasting righteousness. A time of war, and in such a time as this we must take part, line up with God's side, draw the sword, throw away the scabbard and stand true to God and His truth.

Numbers 1:2-4 *"Take ye the sum of all the congregation of the children of Israel, after their families, by the house of their fathers, with the number of their names, every male by their polls; From twenty years old and upward, all that are able to go forth to war in Israel: thou and Aaron shall number them by their armies. And with you there shall be a man of every tribe; every one head of the house of his fathers."*

Here we have the numbers for the holy war. God is calling forth a people who will be strong to fight the good fight of faith and to lay hold on eternal life. The battle of the ages in which the forces of heaven are interlocked with the forces of hell demands the support of those who have dedicated themselves to God and His truth. We are all enlisted. We have all taken the oath of fealty. We have all signed up for this war, God's great holy war. We need the holiness of God so that we might fight this holy war.

The battle is the Lord's and He will have final and full victory. We are to be faithful unto death and Christ will give us the crown of life.

Deuteronomy 3:18 *"And I commanded you at that time, saying, The Lord your God hath given you this land to possess it: ye shall pass over armed before your brethren the children of Israel, all that are meet for the war."*

There can be no release from the binding obligations of this war. In this passage Reuben and Gad and the half tribe of Manasseh wanted to have their heritage on the eastern side of Jordan. As a result, they were given the heritage there on one condition - that they would join faithfully in the battle to procure the rest of the promised land for the other tribes of Israel. In other words, they had to join in unity for the battle. There could be no running away from their obligation to war.

The obligations to war are upon the Christian church. The Christian church is the church of Christ militant on earth. It has battles to fight, victories to be won, land to be possessed and truth to be defended. In such a time as this there can be no opting out, no excuses will be acceptable, and no way to put the responsibilities of the battle onto others, we must all share in the conflict, taking its wounds as well as its victories.

For such a time as this, it is a time of war.

Judges 3: 1-2 *"Now these are the nations which the Lord left, to prove Israel by them, even as many of Israel as had not known all of the wars of Canaan; Only that the generations of the children of Israel might know, to teach them war, at the least such as before knew nothing thereof."*

Here we have the reason for continual conflict. The Christian has to be taught the ways and strategies of the struggle. Those that know not this war must learn it. The obligation upon them is the obligation of God and there is no discharge in this war.

The children of the saints of God must learn that their fathers who fought the early battles of Biblical Christianity in this country and left to them a heritage, that heritage demands protection and defence and the teaching of its principles to coming generations. So let no one put on his bright shining medals and his bright shining uniform because this war is not a war of lounging around the barracks. It is a war to the death, on the front line of the struggle.

That war is increasing and its sacrifices are more demanding as we come nearer to the end of time and the coming of our great God and Saviour Jesus Christ.

Ephesians 6:13-17 *"Wherefore take unto you the whole armour of God, that ye may be able to withstand in the evil day, and having done all, to stand. Stand therefore, having your loins girt about with truth, and having on the breastplate of righteousness: And your feet shod with the preparation of the gospel of peace; Above all, taking the shield of faith, wherewith ye shall be able to quench all the fiery darts of the wicked. And take the helmet of salvation, and the sword of the Spirit, which is the word of God."*

Yes, the armour is provided. Yes, the weapons are provided. Yes, the scene of the battle is set. Yes, the demands of enlistment are spelt out. Now is the time to go to war for God. Now is the time not to be found wanting like those that were found wanting in the day of Jacob's trouble. It was said of them, "On the day that thou stoodest on the other side thou wast like one of them."

The "them" were the traitors. The "them" were the enemies. The "them" signified the opposition to truth and righteousness and redemption.

In such a time as this there is a time and it is the time of war.

A TIME OF PEACE

This is the last significant time, the time of peace. The battles all fought and won, the mountains all climbed and conquered, the rivers all crossed and left behind, and God's inheritance possessed by His people.

This is not the false peace of those who cry and scream and bawl "Peace, peace when there is no peace." This is real peace. This is true peace. This is everlasting peace. This is the peace which Jesus Christ made for us by the blood of His cross.

Joshua 11:23 *"So Joshua took the whole land, according to all that the Lord said unto Moses; and Joshua gave it for an inheritance unto Israel according to their divisions by their tribes. And the land rested from war."*

The great rest day from war comes. It comes to the believer when he has his call to Heaven, Home and God, when he leaves off the armour and his sword to those who are able to grasp it and use it, and crosses over the river of death to be received in the mansions of Heaven.

But there will be rest from war for this old world when Christ, the rider on the white horse as pictured in the apocalypse, shall come as King of kings and Lord of lords for the final redemption of His people and the final claiming of His kingdom.

I Samuel 7:13-14 *"So the Philistines were subdued, and they came no more into the coast of Israel: and the hand of the Lord was against the Philistines all the days of Samuel. And the cities which the Philistines had taken from Israel were restored to Israel, from Ekron even unto Gath; and the coasts thereof did Israel deliver out of the hands of the Philistines. And there was peace between Israel and the Amorites."*

Here we have the end of the conflict, the repossession of the Lord's heritage by His people; the total defeat of their ancient enemies and peace between other traditional enemies because of the fear of the victors that had come into their hearts.

In the battle of life God gives the victory and causes the enemies of God's people to be at peace with them. But that is just a faint picture of the great picture of the future when, as the prophet Isaiah tells us in the second chapter of his prophecy in verse four *"And he shall judge among the nations, and shall rebuke many people: and they shall beat their swords into plowshares, and their spears into pruninghooks: nation shall not lift up sword against nation, neither shall they learn war any more."*

For finally, all God's paths are pleasantness and all His ways are peace.

For such a time as this,

*"Peace, perfect peace, in this dark world of sin
The blood of Jesus whispers peace within."*

May the passion of the redeeming Saviour, the power of the risen Saviour, the peace of the reconciling Saviour, the pardon of the reigning Saviour and the prospect of the returning Saviour be our hope and stay and joy continually.

AMEN AND AMEN!

PHOTOGRAPHS

Rev. and Mrs. J. Kyle Paisley.

A young Ian Paisley on horseback.

Ian and the then Eileen Cassells at Ballyedmond Camp in July 1953.

Dr. Paisley with Rev. Cecil Menary.

The young couple on a visit to London.

Mrs. Paisley pictured at a Christmas Pageant at Ravenhill Free Presbyterian Church. Shepherds include Dr. Bill Woods and the young minister in the foreground is Dr. Bert Cooke.

Free Presbyterian Ministers from left to right:- Revs McVeigh, Greenfield, Elliot, Patrick, McClelland, Paisley, Long, McCrea, Beggs, Beattie, Barnes and Foster.

A packed meeting at the Ulster Hall, Belfast in the 1960s.

Dr. Bob Jones Jr presents an Honorary Doctorate to Rev. Ian Paisley
in the Ulster Hall, 1966.

Mrs. Paisley with Sharon, Rhonda and Cherith during her husband's first imprisonment in 1966.

Visiting Time: The Paisley family outside Crumlin Road prison in 1969.

Dr. Paisley and Rev. Brian Green arriving at the House of Commons, Westminster on 29 June, 1970, when Dr. Paisley took his seat in Parliament.

The Paisley men. Dr. Paisley with twin sons, Ian and Kyle at Kyle's Ordination to the Christian Ministry in 1991.

On the campaign trail.

A TRIBUTE TO
DR. BOB JONES JR

My great and good friend and dear brother in Christ passed on to be with our Lord in November, 1997. How we miss him! At his funeral service in the great University founded by his father, and over which Dr. Bob Jr presided and later became Chancellor, I had the honour to pay him this tribute.

Great grief is never great at talking. The most eloquent speech of grief is a deep silence which can be felt. The tear in the eye trickling on to the cheek, the lump in the husky throat and the pressure of the hand say it all. "Deep calleth unto deep," the Infallible Book records. Yes, in bereavement, the deep of the anguished bereaved calleth unto the deep of the death of our loved one and the billows of inexpressible sorrow surge over our souls.

When I contemplate the death of my beloved friend, Dr Bob, I think of David's lament and tribute to Abner, "Know ye not that there is a prince and great man fallen this day in Israel? And I am this day weak ..." II Samuel 3: 38-39.

I am weak this day, oh so weak, because I will hear no more my brother's voice. Alas, the sound of his voice is now on earth forever still. How I yearn to hear it again. But that cannot be.

ONE: HIS VOICE WAS SOUND IN THE FAITH

Clear and true, it sounded out without apology the great doctrines of the Infallible Word.

In this day of apostasy, when infidelity has captured the pulpit and the teacher's desk, his voice - sound in the faith "once delivered unto the saints" - trumpeted forth.

How it blessed my soul this voice of childlike simplicity and unquestionable loyalty to Holy Scripture!

How many weak and battling souls had their faith renewed and reinvigorated as they heard our brother's voice, unchanging and unchangeable, declare and defend the great fundamentals of the Bible faith?

The summary he wrote, entitled **"The Twentieth Century Magna Carta of Fundamentalism"** which was adopted by the leaders of the World Congress of Fundamentalists as their Declaration, cannot be improved.

A fundamentalist is a born-again believer in the Lord Jesus Christ who:

- Maintains an immovable allegiance to the inerrant, infallible and verbally inspired Bible;

- Believes that whatever the Bible says is so;

- Judges all things by the Bible and is judged only by the Bible and its Revelation is complete;

- Affirms the foundational truths of the historic Christian Faith: The doctrine of the Trinity, The Incarnation, Virgin birth, Substitutionary Atonement, the Bodily Resurrection and Glorious Ascension, and the Second Coming of the Lord Jesus Christ, The New Birth through regeneration of the Holy Spirit, The Resurrection of the saints to life eternal, The Resurrection of the ungodly to final judgment and eternal death, The Fellowship of the Saints, who are the body of Christ;

- Practises fidelity to that Faith and endeavours to preach it to every creature;

- Exposes and separates from all ecclesiastical denial of the Faith, compromise with error, and apostasy from the truth; and

- Earnestly contends for the Faith once delivered.

Surely I know there is a prince and great man fallen this day and I am weak. His sound voice in the faith speaks no more on earth.

TWO: HIS VOICE WAS SWEET IN FORTH-TELLING

Dr Bob was the golden tongue of the twentieth century gospel pulpit.

I never heard him preach the Gospel but I was ashamed of my own pulpit performance. What language! What flow! What eloquence! What sweetness! The secret was not his love for His Lord but rather the Lord's love for him, experienced so richly in his life. Truly the love of Christ constrained him. He loved his Lord because his Lord first loved him.

Samuel Rutherford the Covenanter, said he loved the Lord Jesus most in His red vest - the vesture dipped in blood.

How sweet was Dr Bob's forth-telling of the sacrifice of Christ! How majestic his glorying in the cross!

Truly, he was a precious blood preacher. As he preached much of the blood of redemption, his words were like the stars of the Milky Way in the darkest of nights.

I remember how he delighted to emphasise that the precious blood which he proclaimed fuels the glory of God's everlasting throne. The Lamb as it had been slain in the midst of the throne (Revelation 1:6).

Alas, I am weak this day for that voice so sweet in forth-telling is now silent.

THREE: HIS VOICE WAS STRONG IN THE FIGHT

What a tower of strength his voice was when we engaged the enemies of Christ's Gospel. At his side I have stood as we protested the Church of Rome, the World Congress of Churches, the Ecumenical Evangelism of Billy Graham and others, and those who, for a mess of pottage, sold their Christian birthright. His voice was worth more than a regiment of supporters.

His was the voice of a great man and a royal prince rallying the host of the church militant for the attack. It put strength into the heart, determination into the soul, and dispelled all thoughts of conduct disloyal to the Son of God. Dr Bob was a born leader of men, never sending a young recruit where he would not go himself. It was an honour to serve under him, although all of those who did knew that he made us feel we were rather serving with him because he never showed in any way that we were not his equals (we all knew of course we could never be that).

He has now hung his shield on heaven's wall and studies war no more. In the battlefield I am weak for I will not hear that strong voice in the fight that so encouraged me in the past and rallied the forces of truth.

FOUR: HIS VOICE WAS STRAIGHT IN THE FURORE

The dictionary defines furore as tempest, trouble, rage, uprising, excitement, fury, wildness.

In his life and ministry these were common oppositions for my beloved brother. His long life of 86 years spanned a whole series of the most dramatic and treacherous change in the historic creeds of the churches of Christendom. Churches and schools were constantly changing position. The infidelity of what was wrongly called "modernism" (it was in fact the resurrection of ancient heresies) was followed by the equally false so-called new orthodoxy which was neither new nor orthodox, and fast on the heels of that came a movement going under the flag of "new evangelicalism". This was an evangelicalism which was so bereft of loyalty to the Scripture that it could find fellowship with any brand of self-professed Christianity. The conglomerate has forged itself in ecumenism and charismaticism into a new religion as different from Bible Christianity as chalk is from cheese. Dr Bob's voice was in the midst of this Babel, always straight. For an honest assessment of all the various and invidious attacks on the great fundamentals of historic Christianity it rang out with un- compromising clarity. Billy Sunday used to say that when you hit the bull's eye the bells ring. What deafening ringing of the bells took place as my brother's voice sounded out as a faithful watchman on Zion's walls.

I am this day weak, for when fresh and more vicious satanic attacks are mounted, his straight voice will be so conspicuous by its absence.

FIVE: HIS VOICE WAS SONGFUL IN THE FURNACE

Dr Bob was familiar with the testing of the furnace. He told me on his death bed he still wanted to be useful and he said he had been scribbling some lines.

The furnace drew the best from him, for his voice was always songful in the fire. He was not a singer in the accepted sense but he was ever songful.

In the University's Anniversary Hymn he wrote these lines out of his own experience:

Praise ye Jehovah, from furnace of testing
Fierce though the fire, the Saviour walks there.
Loving, beholding, preserving, enfolding,
From the beginning, till He shall appear.

Alas, alas, I am weak, for his songful voice is beyond my hearing in the choir of the heaven of heavens.

- Dr. Ian R. K. Paisley

DR. BOB JONES III

The worth of a well is judged by the quality of its water.

Ian Paisley's life is a wellspring of flowing water by which so many have been nourished. His family, his church family and his constituent family - those he serves as a member of three Parliaments - Ulster, the United Kingdom and the European community - all drink from this spring. Amazingly there is enough of this spring to provide for all. His life and ministry can only be explained by the providential God-given gifts which he has given back to the Giver to be used for His name's sake.

Since God knit Dr Paisley's heart with my father's heart more than 35 years ago, my family and I have been refreshed by those waters. I find them pure, generous, effervescent, refreshing and healthy for the soul and spirit. Because that is so, let no one who is unprepared to fight say a disparaging word about him in my presence!

His life is a spring of blessing and Christlikeness. The "media" of Christ's day, - the scribes and Pharisees, - published innuendoes, lies and diatribe to discredit Him. Yet the common man heard Him gladly, for He "spake as never man spake" and "as one having authority". Ian Paisley is a truth speaker, and he declares the Lord's truth with boldness. He is heard gladly by those who are too wise to be influenced by liberal media or liberal religion.

No wonder Ian Paisley is loved by hundreds of thousands on both sides of the Atlantic for being the big man with the big heart who serves a big God with big results.

But like every man, he is not only shaped by his God but he is also a composite of those who have interacted with him. The stories and reminiscences shared by Dr Paisley in this book reveal not only what is flowing out of this stream, but also what flowed into it.

The reader will find his faith refreshed and his love for Christ revived. I can say this without fear of contradiction, because I have never found it to be otherwise when in his presence, under his preaching, or reading from his pen.

Here is a spring to swim in and to drink from for all who want to love God more.

Dr. Bob Jones is President of Bob Jones University,
Greenville, South Carolina, USA

DR. KEN CONNOLLY

The very first time I remember meeting Ian Paisley was at a Protestant rally in the Ulster Hall in the city of Belfast.

There was an enormous crowd, it was one of the largest, if not the largest hall in Belfast. It was packed with people. To my recollection, and I could be exaggerating but I don't mean to, I think there might be about 250 seats behind the speaker and those at this time usually occupied by a choir were occupied by the public and every available seat was taken.

My Dad was on the programme, and it was for that reason I was present. One of the other speakers was a young man not much older than I. He stood tall and firm, he had a powerful voice and could have filled that room without any microphones and he spoke with very deep conviction.

He asked a question related to a difference of opinion expressed by the Church of Rome and the Bishop of Quebec - one of them stated salvation was found only in the church of Rome and the other one stated it was possible to be able to go to heaven through another way than by the Church of Rome. He asked the question - "who do we believe?" (A man by the name of Johnnie Cochrane who was an evangelist for the YMCA in Dublin stood up, cupped his mouth and shouted "neither of them, they are both liars" and the whole place went into an uproar of laughter.)

I thought what an uncanny ability that man has. What a powerful memory, he was quoting things from memory that he had been reading in books and magazines and I was very impressed.

I never knew at that moment that I would get the chance to become a friend. We, in fact, started preaching together and we went to the shipyards at lunch time when the men would come out on a nice day and bring their lunches and they would sit around on large pipes by the roadside, and this man and myself would try, with the human voice, to reach those people and tell them the story about Christ.

That was an unusual day. It was a day when my dad - Peter Connolly - a man by the name of Jock Troupe, a man by the name of WP Nicholson, we could mention a lot of them - men who were mightily used of God. The great evangelism of that day was preaching on street corners, and on a Saturday night in the city of Belfast you could have gone to almost any corner of the city and somebody would be proclaiming the Gospel of Christ and they did it with passion and with fervency. Many people came to know Christ.

It was in that environment that I parted from Ian. I came to the United States of America and he stayed to work in his homeland.

I met him sometime later and after I talked to him on the telephone I wondered if he had lost anything he used to have? Is he somewhat different because of what has happened since then? I wondered. I brought him to Universal City and gave him the opportunity of seeing what went on behind the scenes in television land, how films are made and the tricks that are used in order to make these films.

I remember that there were five cars of people. There were about 50 people in each one of these cars and the cars were hooked together and pulled by a tractor. Behind where Ian was sitting was the driver of the tractor and where I was sitting was the guide. The guide had a microphone that linked with all five cars of people and he said to them, "If you look over on the right you will see the room that was used by John Wayne when he made the film *The Cowboys*." At which point Ian, with a voice equivalent said, "John Wayne, a sinner bound for hell unless he is saved by the grace of God". That startled everybody, 250 people looking at him and he and I were sitting at the front. I got embarrassed enough, I would have gladly slipped under the seat if I could have gotten away from the embarrassment. It came to the place where the guide even stopped conversation at points to let Ian get his point in but he preached to them all the way.

I want you to know that was not a special event, that was Ian Paisley wherever he is, under any circumstance that is how he acts.

I remember an occasion when he was in the airport and a businessman was in the company of a large group of business people and saw him, recognised him and said to Ian, "How are you," in a voice that was large enough to fill that part of the airport, where people stopped to listen to what was being said. The reply that Ian gave the businessman was "How am I? I am a sinner saved by grace. I am a child of God, my sins are forgiven. God is my Father, Jesus is my Saviour. I am well, my wife is well, my family is well and you want to know how I am." That is Ian Paisley, and the fervour and the dynamic, the power, the thrust, it is all still there.

As far as I am concerned, though over 40 years have passed in the interval between my first experience and my latter, I see the same man who was that boy that took Belfast by storm with the power and fervency with which he preached the Gospel. I am delighted that he is my friend and I compliment him for God's grace in his life and I encourage those of you who do not know him to enjoy meeting him through the pages of this publication.

On one occasion we were in a prayer meeting before the evening service and I had the privilege of preaching for almost a week at the church he pastored and I remember the fervency of the prayer meeting. You have to experience it in order to appreciate what I am saying. It was so powerful, so convicting. While he was praying he brought his fist down on one of the pews where he was kneeling and it was on the edge of the pew which allowed that portion of it to go down with the power of his fist. The other end came up and actually hit a man on the face. It came up with such a bolt that it knocked the man over, if I remember correctly.

I was in another prayer meeting in that same room and we were all praying and there was a man who always stood to pray and he always threw his fists around when he was praying. As we were all praying together and he was praying, standing and throwing his fists around, a man wanted to pass by to go home. This was an all night of prayer. He did not get past swiftly enough and we heard a tremendous smack and he hit the man on the eye and knocked him out. He went home with a black eye. His wife would not be persuaded that he got a black eye at a prayer meeting!

One other event happened in the time and interval in which Ian and I parted company to go to different parts of the vineyard to minister and I watched on television one night when Ian as a member of the European Parliament which was being addressed by the Pope, objected to the Pope's presence. I suddenly heard on the news the voice of my friend, as familiar as it was, and he was informing the Pope that he was not the Vicar of Christ on earth but that he was the antichrist. Men came to take Ian out of the room and as they got on either side of him he gave no resistance but they had to hold him up and pull him at the same time. His heels were on the carpet and all the time that he was leaving the room he was addressing the Pope and telling him that he was not one of his disciples and he believed he would stand in serious judgment on the Day of Judgment before God.

I had come back from the United States and was doing some visiting in different parts of England, Scotland and Ireland, meeting some of my old friends and my journey took me to the city of Belfast. I remember meeting Ian on that occasion and he was pastoring in what we refer to as the old church. It was the one before they built Martyrs Memorial and it was the place where many people came to know Christ and people were encouraged in the faith.

(I remember being invited to those meetings and we had great meetings. I am referring to those meetings in which the incident happened in the prayer room). My friend Vivien Laird who was with me at the time was invited also to be a part of this ministry and he was shocked beyond belief. He could not imagine that another Presbyterian like Ian Paisley would have conducted himself in the way he did. He did not have any disagreements with Ian but he was shocked to find out that that was the kind of witness and ministry going on in his life. It greatly influenced Vivien and he became a missionary and spent his life in Egypt doing mission work and is now home in retirement.

I was in the ministry in which I was trying to put some things on video tape that I thought should be shared with God's people. One of the things which influenced me was my conversation with Ian on the subject of revival. Ian told me what the revival was like in 1859. He had given it very serious and deep study and had written a book on it, called 'The '59 Revival'. He was able to tell me the names of the people who were involved and what their relationships were with each other and how the revival spread from one community to another community. After listening for some considerable time to him describing all of this I said to him, "Ian, that has got to go on video tape. You should honestly pray that God would give you the means and the influence to put that on video tape and share that testimony with other people." His response to that was, "Ken, you need to do it." I said, "But Ian I don't know the story like you know the story." His reply to that was, "Oh yes you will, because I have written on it and I will give you whatever other written material you need and you can get all the information in this book on the revival of 1859." I am indebted. When that film was made it was made on location in different parts of Ireland, and every place we went Dr Paisley went there with me, and every time I gave commentary he evaluated my commentary and gave me suggestions and I am greatly indebted to him.

He is a student of books as well as of history. He has a mammoth library and I don't know anybody among my circle of friends, today who has a library as large as his. It is not just simply a collection of books. He can tell you what message lies in every book. He can tell you where that book is, on what shelf it lies, what colour it is, how far away from the end. I was with him in England when he wanted to get a book which he wanted to give to me. I said, "There is no time to do it Ian because we will be parted company before it can get here." He said, "No, it will be here in the morning." He called up his daughter, told her what colour the book was, what aisle the book was on, how high up, what shelf she would find it and everything that she needed to know. The next morning, as he promised, the book was right there.

He is a profound student and reader and he can tell you more than I know of everybody else who has the ability to record it. He can tell you more about God's dealings in past days with various men, what their weaknesses and strong points were, and he not only has a tremendous ability to read but he has a tremendous ability to memorise what he has read. He can cite, almost verbatim, many of the things which come from books which he has read years ago.

Before I conclude I ought to say that what impresses me about Ian Paisley is not his courage, it is not the power of his voice, it is not the abilities of his mind, it is how he loves the Saviour. How he talks about Him. How in moments, when we are alone, we pray together and his heart is broken before God and he is praying in earnestness for another visitation from heaven with revival power. When you sit in the car with him on the way to a meeting and he has got his Bible on his lap getting his heart ready to preach to people and he leans over and shares some spiritual truth with you which he has just found in the Book and when he is talking about it his eyes are wet. He loves the Saviour and that is why I love him. It is that love of Christ more than anything else around Ian Paisley's life that has impressed me and has caused me to fall more deeply in love with my Saviour at the same time.

Dr. Ken Connolly, California, USA.

DR. ROD BELL

I have had the privilege of "walking with giants". I feel greatly blessed to have been in the presence of great men like Dr Bob Jones Sr, Dr Gilbert Stenholm, Dr Bob Jones Jr, Dr Bob Jones III, Dr Harold B Sightler, Dr Noel Smith, and Dr Oliver B Greene. So often I feel like a "wee sapling" among the giant redwoods. The influence of great men upon my life has had a dramatic effect. I've seen such men in all types of situations.

One of the biggest giants to me is Ian Paisley from Ulster. I first became acquainted with Dr Paisley while I was a student at Bob Jones University. Dr Bob Jones Jr had this big man who had been in jail to come and preach in chapel. I was fascinated, not only with his stature and his accent (his Northern Ireland brogue), but I was especially intrigued by this man's message. It was the freshness of heaven upon his life, in the reality of the resurrected Christ whom he magnified, that won and captured my heart.

I thought, "This man must be an independent Baptist because no Presbyterian preaches like that. Presbyterians in our country are dead, cold, fossilized, and apostate."

But when I met him, he said, "I am a Free Presbyterian; I've been set free from all of that, my brother."

Most people in the world do not know the Ian Paisley that I know. The world doesn't know the compassionate, hard-hitting, Christ-honouring, spirit-filled, loving, honest man I know. The press has always tried to make Dr Paisley look like a villain, but I've found that every time they try to make him look bad, God makes him look good. He has the spirit of the reformers and the prophets of old. I've enjoyed being with him and Dr Bob Jr in India, the Philippines, Singapore, Korea, Hungary, Australia, Africa, Canada, and all over America. What a joy it has been to travel with those two "giants" and just be a tag-along.

I've had the privilege of being with him in the heat of the battle. He's allowed me to stay in his home, and his family has treated me as one of their own. His precious wife, Eileen, has a wit and humour that sustains her through the tremendous stress and pressure she withstands because of the situation in Northern Ireland. She supports her husband 100 percent; she is truly a "help-meet" to him. He could not do the job he's called to do without her beside him. She is of sterling silver - a precious ruby. When Ian got her, he got the ruby of rubies.

You learn much about a man's family when you stay in his home and see his children. All the Paisley children love the Lord and are faithfully serving Him in various capacities. His twin sons, Kyle and Ian Jr, are a blessing to be around. Ian Jr, is an astute intelligent politician with the wit and conviction of his dad. Kyle, a preacher, has the keen insight and expository genius of his dad. I believe Kyle will be a great leader in the Free Presbyterian movement. I've had him to speak in our Congresses several times, and I've had the privilege of speaking in his church. We've travelled and preached together in South America. It is clear to me that Dr Paisley's "preaching mantle" has fallen upon Kyle.

I shall never forget the first time Dr Paisley came to our church in 1970. Our new auditorium was packed, and there had been bomb threats because of Dr Paisley's visit. The ecumenists were angry because we were taking a stand for the Word of God and the testimony of Jesus Christ. One evening, I answered the phone; the caller said, "The hatemonger from Northern Ireland will not live to get out of Virginia Beach."

I immediately called the police. The next thing I knew, we had the city police, the state police, the SWAT team, and the FBI come. There were six or seven undercover policemen assigned to Dr Paisley. They chauffeured him wherever he went and checked for bombs under the cars, using dogs and special mirrors. They sat and guarded his hotel room all night. I went down to pick him up the next morning and as I started to knock on the door, some policemen stepped out from behind the bushes. Before I knew it, I was "spread eagled". They made me identify myself, and I told them I was the preacher, Rod Bell. I had to show them some identification before I could get my speaker. This was the beginning of a long and fruitful relationship with one of God's choicest servants. I have never been around Dr Paisley or the Free Presbyterians that I did not develop a greater hunger for the Word of God, a greater desire to pray, and a greater love for the Lord Jesus.

One of my first trips with Ian Paisley was to find the first missionary who came to America, who landed on Virginia's Eastern Shore. I asked Dr Paisley, "A Presbyterian, Calvinist missionary? Coming as a missionary to win souls? Oh, come on! A five-pointer with a burden for missions?"

He said, "Forget the buttons, preach the whole garment - Christ died for sinners. Ah, yes, he's here somewhere. We've got to find him."

Early one morning we got in the car, crossed the twenty-five miles across the Chesaspeake Bay Bridge to Virginia's Eastern Shore, and travelled to Accomack, Virginia. We spent several hours inquiring in the town, but no one knew anything of a "Francis Makemie". Finally, we found an old Presbyterian librarian.

"Yes. There's a marker, way out in the countryside here, but I doubt you'll be able to find it."

Dr Paisley, like a bloodhound on the trail of a criminal, said, "We'll find it."

Off we went, out through the countryside, down trails, through the undergrowth. We found an old Presbyterian graveyard. As we walked around through the bushes and twigs, it was like a jungle, we found a statue of the first missionary the Presbyterians ever sent to America to evangelise the colonies. The man's name was Francis Makemie, and the inscription gave the town and the date. We prayed, and Dr Paisley prayed for God to keep evangelistic zeal and to give us a heart for souls like Makemie. Rod Jr, a lad of just fourteen said, "Dad, I'll never forget this day." We stood there in the rain, where the history of this great man had almost been forgotten. Someone had taken a rifle and shot off half of the face from Makemie's statue. (Today, 1999, they have restored this statue and made a memorial park for this first Presbyterian missionary to America on the Eastern Shore. The park is lovely - visit it sometime.)

Paisley said, "That's the devil's crowd. Even though he's dead, they're still taking shots at him! That's what they'll do to you and me, too, Rod, after we pass through this vale of tears and sorrow. They'll take potshots at us."

Another time, Dr Paisley and I met in Washington DC for an extremely important appointment with Senators Strom Thurmond and Jesse Helms. Our appointment was for 4.00 in the afternoon so we had the whole day to sight-see. I asked Dr Paisley where he'd like to go.

"I'd like to see the Arlington House, Robert E Lee's home, and the place where he stood when he made his decision to fight for the South instead of the North."

"I don't know if there is such a place."

"Oh, yes there is. I've read about it in the history books. Let's go."

We got on a bus to Arlington Cemetery and went over to the Arlington House, made our way through the crowd, went to the caretaker, and asked him to show us the place.

He said, "There is one window where it is said that Robert E Lee stood where he could look across the Potomac River and see the White House and up Pennsylvania Avenue to the Capitol."

Dr Paisley asked, "Would you mind if I just went over there and stood for a few minutes?"

"Of course. Please do."

Doc usually got to do what he wanted because of his public stature - people knew who he was. They let down the rope, and he went over to the window and stood, with his head bowed. He stood in silence; I could tell he was praying. After a few minutes, he came back, and we viewed the rest of the house. Later in the day, I asked him, "Doc, why was that the place you were most interested in?"

"I wanted to stand in the footsteps of a man who had courage, and who had enough courage to turn down the opportunity to become the Chief Staff Officer of the United States Army and go with the Confederacy - not because it was popular, but because he had conviction. I always admire a man with conviction, and I wanted to thank God for a man named Robert E Lee who had conviction. God, give us men today who, like Robert E Lee, have convictions."

I've had the privilege for over twenty-five years of speaking at the Great Easter Convention at the Martyrs Memorial Free Presbyterian Church in Northern Ireland. What a privilege to be identified with a man and people who are not ashamed of the gospel of the grace of God, who have such a great zeal for souls and a world-wide missionary outreach and who stand without apology against the one-world church and the mother of harlots, the Roman Catholic system.

The highlight of the Belfast Easter Convention, of course, is always what I call, "Dr Paisley's state of the union address." He preaches in the afternoon and gives the "challenge" for another year. The first time I saw the closing service of the convention, there were three thousand people standing and singing "God Be With You 'Till We Meet Again," waving white handkerchiefs.

The Free Presbyterians are a praying people. During my darkest peril, my son Rod Jr, called Dr Paisley and told him I was in a bad way and that the doctors were not expecting me to live. Dr Paisley went to the Lord in prayer. The next day, he called my wife and told her that God had given him the assurance that I was going to live. The Lord gave him the assurance from the Word of God: "Epaphroditus, my brother ... was sick nigh unto death: but God had mercy on him; and not on him only, but on me also, lest I should have sorrow upon sorrow." (Phil. 2:25-27).

The Free Presbyterians took me to the Lord in prayer. I received phone calls, letters, gifts, cards, and encouragement from all over Northern Ireland, Canada, and Australia from Free Presbyterian brethren who were praying. Still today I see them, and they tell me they have held me up in prayer daily. I believe it, the power of prayer is evident in their lives and ministries.

In April of 1990, after my recovery, I again had the joy of speaking in the great Easter Convention,. How wonderful it was to be able once again to preach and fellowship with our brethren of like precious faith! It was unusual the way that I felt through that time of recovery. I thought that if I could just get together with the brethren of like precious faith - if I could get around good, fundamental, Bible-believing men who loved the Lord, I would be better, I would be stronger. God taught me a lesson: we draw strength one from another. We need to be encouragers and encourage those who are going through times of difficulty. I thank the Lord for that experience.

The schedule of the Easter Convention is not one you cherish. It is one that keeps you on the go and one that causes time to go by quickly. Those involved seem to forget when to go to bed and when to eat. We have enjoyed many good meals in Mrs Paisley's kitchen, at 1.00 or 2.00 in the morning after services all day.

Dr Ken Connolly and I had the privilege of speaking in the Crumlin Road Prison. There were over twelve hundred prisoners, many in for murder. This is the prison where Dr Paisley had been incarcerated. He showed me his "suite" as we preached in there one Sunday morning. To see these men raise their hand for prayer and to see the power of God resting upon Dr Connolly and Dr Paisley as they preached was a unique experience. I had the joy of preaching in the prison from Matthew 11:28-30, "Come unto me, all ye that labour and are heavy laden, and I will give you rest."

Preaching on the street corners and in the city squares in Belfast is one of the joys of going to Northern Ireland. As the accordion is played, songs are sung, testimonies given; then the Word of God is preached. There is a solemn stirring among the crowded streets of Belfast. The first time I preached there, the policemen instructed me, "If a motorcycle comes by and there are two men on the motorcycle, the one on the back will be the one doing the shooting, so hit the deck!"

Then they turned me loose and told me to go ahead and preach.

I thought, "Dear Lord, how can I ever get my mind off the motorcycle and on the Master?" But God enabled me to preach, and I had a great time and great liberty.

I honestly believe that I have been in every old bookstore in the British Isles and Northern Ireland. If any town has an old bookstore, Dr Paisley knows where it is. We were in a bookstore in Northern Ireland during a time when terrorism was rampant and bombings were frequent. We were on the floor, looking through the books, and a great blast went off down the street People began to run and look to see what was happening. I got up and headed toward the door too.

Just then, Doc said, "Look, Rod. I think I found a good book. Look here!"

He found a volume for which he had been searching a long time. "There may be another one or two around here."

We kept searching while everyone else was scampering to see what the bomb blasts were about. Here was a man who was more interested in books than the blast! I can't say I was ever that excited about a book. All I wanted to do was to get out of there in a hurry! But I never showed my concern to him; we just kept looking for books. Later, we found out that the IRA had blown up a nearby car.

During one trip to the Easter Convention, I had just arrived when we visited a policeman whose arms had been blown off by an IRA terrorist bomb. We visited with him in the hospital - a young man who had been brutally maimed for life because of the brutality and senseless killings of the IRA.

The same day we visited the family of another man who had been blown up by a bomb. Paisley went to give his condolences. One of the constables came and said, "What are you doing here, Dr. Paisley? Don't you know this is not a good place to be? This is not a secure place!"

Dr. Paisley replied, "These people are in my political area, and I have come to pray and offer my help to the bereaved."

The constable persisted, "Don't you know that man was making a bomb and it exploded prematurely and killed him?"

"His family need prayer."

We prayed and Doc prayed that God would save the family of this man.

The thing that has impressed me most about Dr Paisley is that he always tells the truth. He is known as a man of his word. There is not a hair on his head that has even a hint of compromise. "The Big Man" (as they call him in Ulster) tells the truth, unlike our politicians today. The reason Dr Paisley is so popular among his constituents, even the Roman Catholics in his constituency, is that they know he always tells the truth.

He is a man of great prayer, and he walks with the Lord. We have, in my sixty-four years, seen the truth become a lie and a lie become the truth. Right is wrong, and wrong is right. The Deceiver is capturing the hearts of men. Truth is slain in the streets.

But thank God our God is faithful, and He will send revival: "If my people, which are called by My name, shall humble themselves and pray ..." As I heard the cry of the old-timers in Northern Ireland when they bowed to pray, "Oh God! Remember '59. Remember '59," so may we pray for revival. The great Fulton Street prayer meeting swept across the nation, and gave birth to the Second Great Awakening. It was an awakening of prayer because of the great economic and apostate conditions that existed in that day. May we get our heads out of the sand and beg God, "Do it again, Lord." As we face the twenty-first century, it is our only hope.

Dr. Rod Bell, Tabernacle Baptist Church, Virginia Beach is President of the Fundamental Baptist Fellowship of America.

DR. BRIAN GREEN

It was in 1963 that I first heard of Ian Paisley. A colleague, who had been with me at Bible College, had visited Ulster and gone to the Ravenhill Free Presbyterian Church to hear their renowned preacher, and immediately felt I had a lot in common with him. He recommended me - even though he was never of the same persuasion himself. At the same time Dr Paisley had read a pamphlet that I had co-authored, encouraging all Baptists not to go into the WCC. He wrote to me (the only letter I had ever received from IRKP) inviting me to his annual Easter Convention. I had just settled into my second pastorate and counted it a privilege to be invited to preach in Northern Ireland and so I gladly accepted. Immediately this was known in my congregation there was opposition, which was a great surprise to me. I had delegations from far and wide to try and persuade me not to go to Ulster and associate with such a notorious man! I was warned that my going there might prejudice a promising career! The more opposition I received the more I determined I was to see for myself. What a blessing that God gave me foresight to persist because that was the beginning of a great adventure in the work for God.

FIRST VISIT

On the Easter Sunday after finishing my evening service I was taken to the airport to catch the five to twelve plane for Belfast. I had never flown before and my fears were increased when we were told there would be a delay and subsequently we would have to land in Dublin because of the bad weather at Nutts Corner, Belfast. I thought it was an IRA plot, but I was relieved that our visit to Dublin only lasted less than an hour. In the early hours of the morning I first met Dr Paisley and from that moment a very real personal friendship developed.

The first visit was full of incidents which convinced me that "Doc" was a man sent from God for such a time as this. The visit wasn't without its surprises! like talking all night and then being given half an hour to sleep before setting out for the prayer meeting before the morning Convention meetings. I recall with great pleasure listening at the Convention to Dr Paisley's father, to Willie Mullan and a man called Davies (the wee man from Wales) who seemed to get a lot of verbal "stick" because he taught heresy in the South Wales College where Dr Paisley attended.

During that visit I was shown eight Free Presbyterian Churches that I had been informed in London, before I left, did not exist, and I observed at first hand the mighty power and unction upon God's man. I came home determined to experience something of the power the "big man" showed to make a stand for God and truth.

It was during one of my early visits to the Province that I preached at one of the tent meetings with Dr Paisley on a Sunday afternoon. After the service many people came up to me to express their appreciation for the message and I well remember one man coming up to me and saying "what a powerful preacher the big man is - do you know when he preaches he can spit to the fifteenth row!" I knew I could never be that good a preacher. With this great man, witnessing his amazing preaching ability in many places and countries of the world, which I am sure would not have been mine had the providence of God not brought us together. Early in our association we decided to form a body to stand against the prevailing religious ills of our day. Romanism had become resurgent after

143

many years of being dormant. Modernistic and liberal unbelief had permeated the churches and the theological colleges, and false religions were creeping into our land. There was a deadness about evangelicals which brought about an impotency to deal with the situation. The British Council of Protestant Christian Churches was formed and its natural leader was Dr Paisley. God has given him that rare gift of being accepted as a man apart, and yet a man of the people who can be trusted and followed through thick and thin.

PROTESTS

Together we spoke at the famous Oxford Union debate against Romanist St John Stevas and a high church Canon of the Church of England. Together we have stood in protest against compromise and evil outside St Paul's Cathedral where we were pelted with tomatoes and eggs! Outside Westminster Abbey where the Jesuit "Father" Thomas Corbishley was the first Romanist to preach there since the Reformation; to Uppsala in Sweden protesting at the World Council of Churches Assembly; in London and Glasgow at the Pope's visit and in Liverpool at the giving over of JC Ryle's Cathedral pulpit to the Roman Catholic Archbishop. Perhaps our most memorable protest was in Rome, when on two occasions we followed a treacherous Archbishop of Canterbury (Ramsey and Runcie) to expose to the world the evil of so-called Protestant leaders' compromise in recanting on the glorious Reformation. On our first protest in Rome, we travelled on the same plane as Archbishop Ramsey. At first he thought we were part of his delegation (we were wearing clerical attire) but then he recognised Dr Paisley and refused to move from his seat, fearing we would do him harm! On our arrival at Rome airport Dr Paisley and Rev John Wylie were refused entry and my abiding memory as I reluctantly left the airport is of the great volume of noise spoken very plainly for all in the airport to understand, "I am a British subject!"

It seems to me that Dr Paisley's forthright leadership down the years has stemmed the tide of corruption within the church, and has alerted many to the dangers that have confronted us.

HIGH LEIGH

It was in 1987 that we began our annual High Leigh Holiday Bible Conference. From the outset and in every succeeding year Dr and Mrs Paisley have been the leaders, and their presence has been a great blessing and encouragement to countless numbers, including my wife Pat and myself. High Leigh is Ian Paisley at his best, and so many fighting a lonely battle have found strength through his ministry to go on. Others have been enlightened to separate themselves from compromising denominations and have always found in Dr. Paisley a sympathetic hearing of their difficulties.

THE CRYPT

The meetings in the Crypt of the House of Commons have been other occasions to assemble large numbers to hear God's man deliver his soul on some important theme affecting 20th Century Christianity.

I still remember that day I drove Dr Paisley to the House of Commons for his first day as an MP. They did not like him and made it known with their sneers, laughs and hissing. I confess to being scared - but not the "big man" from Ulster. He was "as bold as a lion". Things have changed since that day thirty years ago, Dr Paisley is now a respected elder statesman, but his views have not altered and we have much to thank God for when we realise He has put someone in the high places of our land with the holy fire burning within him.

HIS JOY

Pat and I have always counted it a special privilege to have Dr Paisley stay in our home whilst he is in London. We are honoured by his presence, his kindly manner and his constant joyful spirit. He never seems to be down, and is always laughing even in the thick of problems and trouble. Mind you, I am not sure about his singing in the morning! Sometimes when he needs to catch an early plane to either Belfast or Brussels he will rise as bright as a button, singing joyful hymns. Now I come from the land of singing but how can you be so bright and sing even before the birds have finished their dawn chorus?

Nobody can explain Ian Paisley apart from the power and provision of God in giving to us for such a time as this, this Person, Pastor, Preacher, Politician and Publisher all found in one man. Not to mention the many other facets of his remarkable character.

Dr. Brian Green is the Minister of Calvary Free Grace Baptist Church, Feltham, England and is General Secretary of the British Council of Protestant Christian Churches.

DR. JOHN DOUGLAS

In the autumn of 1962, Belfast was abuzz with the statement released from the Pulpit of Ravenhill Free Presbyterian Church.

Rev Ian R K Paisley had declared that he would travel to the Vatican to take a stand there along with two other ministers, Rev John Wylie and Rev John Douglas. Stillness fell on the whole congregation as they listened to the suspense-filled announcement. Three Protestant ministers from Belfast would go to Rome to protest at the second Vatican Council! The reason for this controversial witness unfolded itself in that never-to-be-forgotten Sunday night statement.

Churchmen from historic Protestant denominations all over the world, but notably from the USA and Britain, had been invited as observers to this showpiece of sacredotalist clericalism in the Vatican. They were to make this pilgrimage ostensibly for the purpose of listening in and fraternising with the prelates of Rome as purportedly ground breaking pronouncements came to be agreed at the Vatican, before their very eyes, as it were. It was thought there would be a dramatic shift in Vatican policy, especially in relation to other Christians. They anticipated great things, The wind of change had begun to blow, they believed, through the musty corridors of that ancient institution on the banks of the Tiber. The event promised a new face for the Church of Rome. The intransigent was becoming beneficent. The advocates of church unity had dreamed of this for years! Words like *koinonia* (fellowship), love, oneness, grew in significance and popularity. For the Pope, who could be relied on to speak of himself as Peter and the Vicar of Christ, to actually make mention of them as separated brethren, just melted their hearts completely. These visiting churchmen were beside themselves with joy.

But the whole thing had been shrewdly calculated as a masterly gambit in episcopal control. It was a colossal exercise in Roman Catholic ecumenism. These churches could be ecumenical, they could be one but they had to unite under the authority of the papacy. The sell out of participating denominations had begun in earnest.

Now three Free Presbyterian ministers were going to Rome to put the protest back into Protestantism.

Soon the time came to board the aircraft. The feelings of John Wylie, a benign soul, were deeply stirred as he pressed on ahead of the other two. He hurried on through an assortment of nuns and priests. The airport seemed filled with them. John audibly offered the prayer, "Thank God for Ulster. Thank God for the reformation and the reformers." and he whistled a little tune. It was not, "God Who had made the daisies."

Congenial stewardesses placed us in a special cabin at the front where space had been reserved for all the clergy. When we were all in our seats, one of the very important dignitaries - with the emphasis upon the nit - arose from his place at the front. Smiling like a fox who had just had a visit from some tasty fat chickens, he complemented those who had travelled. He welcomed all his ecumenical brethren, he was especially glad to see so many in their clerical garb, and hoped that their spiritual aspirations would be fulfilled in this visit to the eternal city. John's quiet little voice carried up to the front. He said his hope was completely different. He placed his trust alone in Christ and in His finished work. He did not trust in clerical orders or clerical garb to save him. For some reason this did not please the noble bishop. He retorted, "You do not look over-righteous yourself."

John's motor was firing now on all cylinders. He entered into the fray at once. He said, "That's right. I found out years ago that my righteousness could not save me. I had to come to Christ as a guilty lost sinner and cry to Him for mercy. I had to seek the cleansing of His precious blood that washes whiter than snow. Now I am justified by faith in Him alone, by that act of God's free grace, wherein He pardoneth all our sins and accepteth us as righteous in His sight, only for the righteousness of Christ imputed to us, and received by faith alone." The Bishop sat down deflated, without a word. All these men had heard the Gospel, succinctly put before them in that simple, rapid-fire testimony.

We reached Rome in the late afternoon, the three of us ventured forth to take a little stroll before dark. Mr Paisley had an idea. "Let us walk to the Vatican."

John stopped a passer-by. "Can you tell me the way to the Vatican?" (Now there is a tendency with the Ulsterman, if he is not understood due to language difficulties, to raise his voice somewhat. It is just surprising how often this little technique is used. It appears to be so successful. It is a wonder that language schools have not tried it long ago.) John raised his voice a little. He repeated his question - to no avail. "yes," he said explaining things further, "we want to see the Pope. You know, the antichrist, the beast - for we have come to dung him out."

Maybe it is as well the raising of the voice did not work.

We did not reach the Vatican that night.

With the help of an American Missionary named Ray, a large amount of Scripture portions in Italian had been obtained. With these in their possession, the three Free Presbyterian Ministers descended on St Peter's Square. People thronged that square gladly receiving the Scriptures in their own mother tongue. These portions included the Gospel of John and the Epistle of Peter.

Ken, a British missionary working locally, accompanied us to help with distribution and assist with any language problems which might arise. The tract distribution did not continue in the Square as long as we expected. Like the Psalmist we were compassed about like bees. The plain-clothes agents of the Vatican came by to take our names. They intended to confiscate the Scriptures used in the distribution. They looked about and they searched painstakingly for the whole supply of this Scripture literature but they could not find it.

Now we were not a big help to them, but the upshot of this was that we had to leave Vatican Square and enter the neighbouring thoroughfare called, inappropriately, Reconciliation Street. In this street, too, there was confrontation. A Jesuit Priest tried to stop Mr Paisley handing out these Scriptures. "Protestanti," we heard him shout, repeatedly. He wanted the people to throw the Word of God down on the street. But for all his fuming, his shouting, his fierce gesticulations, most of the people turned a deaf ear to him. They wisely held on to their Bible portions. What a day that was. Monks, nuns, dignitaries, the common people - all alike had the written, life-giving Word put into their hands. About five thousand copies of the Word of God were given to the people that day, within yards of the Vatican and within sight of the Pope's personal quarters. Who knows what may come of those efforts?

We went back to our hotel rooms feeling very pleased that we had begun our activities in Rome with the distribution of the Word of Life.

Next morning brought a different complexion to our experience. We were promptly locked in a Police van and whisked away to Police Headquarters for interrogation. On the way there we lustily sang some great salvation hymns.

"I'm not ashamed to own my Lord" and its rousing chorus "At the Cross," especially rang out triumphantly. The singing was tremendous. Now, these many years later, it is still embedded in the memory.

We were kept in detention for nearly three hours, and were forbidden to give out any more literature, forbidden to return to the Vatican and forbidden to enter any property belonging to the Church. Three police officers accompanied us everywhere we went from that time on.

Well, we concluded, if we cannot witness to the people we can witness to our guards. At least the police cannot get away. Each minister put an Italian Bible on a policeman's knee, turned over the pages from passages like Isaiah 53 to Romans 3, and from John 3, to I John 1:7 and John 6:37. These and other verses were read by our official companions. We prayed the devil would overstep himself and that the Word of God would bear fruit to eternal life.

It was almost time to return home. We had witnessed, before the police caught up with us we had seen at first hand tragic evidence of the emptiness, the superstition, the error of the Roman Catholic system. Mr Paisley, who had his homework exceptionally well done, amazed his two friends by taking us on an unforgettable tour of the religious sites of Rome. We looked at the plaster facade of one chapel in Rome. It portrayed the miraculous removal of the Holy House of Nazareth to Loretto. The angels carried it off all in one piece from Galilee to save it from the infidel, we are told. This house has had strange whims. With the reputation of a vagrant, it has been known to shift its location once in a while. It takes a roving fit and journeys on when the rent is bad. Then there was St Maggiore, the biggest basilica in Rome dedicated to the Virgin Mary. Here the effigy of Mary hangs on the cross, to suggest that Mary as the co-redemptrix had a part in atoning for our sins. Inside, above the altar, the Lord is depicted removing the crown from His own head and placing it on the head of the Virgin. She is crowned with the diadem of Christ Himself and so made the Queen of Heaven. We watched as people came for pardon. They genuflected before the Confessional. Then, while these worshippers were still kneeling, the two doors of the box suddenly swung open and the little bonneted priest, like the emerging figure in the cuckoo clock, bobbed forward with a fishing rod in his hand. He promptly struck these unfortunates around the head with this rod as if he was trying to beat some sense into them. He did not beat too hard because to do so meant the flow of money would stop. They will claim that the rod is a replica of Peter's. That rod, you remember, was the one used to catch the fish with the money. Ever since, priests have tried to imitate and perpetuate what he did. The fish is different nowadays. There is no truth in the rumour that the fish is of the sucker variety.

We lost part of a film we had made when the police confiscated the roll because of an attempt to photograph a poster for the concluding message. That picture would have to be taken at Belfast Airport. There Mr Paisley reported to the 'press'. The poster was then displayed in its vivid colour and unmistakable message. It drew a clear line of demarcation between the apostasy of the WCC and the separated stand of vigorous and Biblical Protestantism. Mr Paisley repeated the words of II Cor 6:14 to 18, called for an immediate response to the challenge of God's Word. There was no future in compromise. God's Word demanded obedience now.

However, we were able to get large footage which we later showed to packed congregations all over Ulster.

A special Welcome Home Rally arranged for the Ulster Hall drew a full house. People at home, hearing of our arrest in Rome, had prayed, their interest intensified by this bold venture for God. At the rally the audience listened with rapt attention, responding at times with laughter or with thunderous applause.

Other rallies were held across the Province. Thousands were stirred. Those meetings in some sense laid the foundation for the revival rallies of 1966 and after.

We are thankful for Dr Paisley's vision, his courage and commitment to the cause of God and truth both then and now. For his personal ministry and that given by the Lord to the Free Presbyterian Church, we praise the Lord that it has come for such a time as this. May the Saviour enable it to continue a faithful and resounding witness into the days to come.

Dr. John Douglas ministered in our Portavogie, Moneyslane and Lisburn Churches. He is Clerk of Presbytery and Principal of the Whitefield College of the Bible.

DR. ALAN CAIRNS

It is almost fifty years since I first met Dr. Paisley. Of course, I was just a boy then! During that time I have known him as a preacher, a teacher, an evangelist, a church administrator and a friend. I have been close to him in public controversy and in private prayer, in the church, and in the fellowship of his family.

He is not perfect, is often demanding, and can at times be so absorbed in his own thoughts that he can look you in the eye and fail to recognise you! I first found this out when travelling one day with him and his wife. Mrs. Paisley was telling him something of interest and he was apparently listening. But only apparently, for after a few minutes he turned to her and said, 'Brother, let me tell you....' Mrs. Paisley rolled her eyes at me, and we both laughed. That brought the big man out of his reverie and he wondered why we were so amused!!

Having watched Dr. Paisley closely in so many varied settings over so many years I have to say that towering over every other characteristic is the simple but profound fact that he is a man of God. This is what so many 'outside' estimates of the man can never fathom. Ian Paisley's religion is not something assumed or adopted as a cover for an ulterior purpose. It is real. The more intimately you get to know him the more you realize that here is a man who knows God and is in vital touch with God.

He is a man of one Book. Though he has a vast and well-used library, he judges every book of man by the Book of God. He is a master of the English Bible and in conversation is constantly scattering gems he has found in his reading of the Word.

He is a man of powerful prayer. I have never known anyone who can plead the power of the blood of Christ for victory in prayer as he can. I can look back on times when the Holy Spirit came down as he prayed, and the gathered company were lifted heavenward.

He is a man with a mighty passion for souls. He lives to preach the gospel and to point men to Christ. He is a committed Calvinist, but as he states in his commentary on Romans chapter 9, the doctrine of election is no deterrent to a passion for souls. God gave him that passion and has blessed his ministry to the salvation of thousands.

Dr. Paisley is a man of unwavering Protestant principles. While others have abandoned or modified their stand for the Reformed Faith, he has stood fast.

A theologian and historian of no mean ability, he knows the great doctrinal issues at stake in the controversy with Rome and has never wavered in his commitment to the cause of God's truth, however unpopular his stand may be.

Most of all, however, Dr. Paisley is a lover of the Lord Jesus Christ. That is the key to his entire life. Love for Christ because of Christ's love for him is what drives him. Faithfulness to Christ is the foundation of his ministry.

I count it a privilege to be his friend and colleague. No one can know Ian Paisley as I have, without being the better for it, without being stirred to follow the Lord more fully and more faithfully.

I thank my God upon every remembrance of him and salute him as a man God called to the kingdom for such a time as this.

Dr. Alan Cairns is the Minister of Faith Free Presbyterian Church,
Greenville, South Carolina, USA.

DR. S. B. COOKE

The scriptures declare that "none of us liveth unto himself". In that respect Ian Paisley has had a profound and lasting influence on my Christian life.

We met for the first time fifty years ago in a small prayer meeting in what was then known as Ravenhill Evangelical Mission Church. I had been saved a few weeks earlier in a gospel campaign conducted by a Canadian evangelist, Oswald J. Smith and, acting upon advice from my Mother, I began to attend Dr. Paisley's church.

Looking back, it was a defining moment with regard to my future work and service for God. We became firm friends. With my cousin John Douglas, who is now the Principal of the Whitefield College of the Bible, we travelled with him on numerous occasions to his many evangelistic meetings, in a variety of second-hand cars of indeterminate age and condition. (Traffic was light in those days - no MOT, not even a driving test!)

His devotion to Christ and powerful preaching of the gospel, allied to a fervent stand against ecumenism and the Church of Rome, made a deep impression upon me and served as an inspiration for my own ministry to which I was called shortly afterwards. Down these many years I have greatly valued his friendship and fellowship.

As a colleague in the Lord's work I have noted with admiration his qualities of leadership and depth of wisdom in the many commitments, responsibilities and complex problems of church life. We have shared many platforms together. I have witnessed at close quarters his many gifts and talents as a soul-winning evangelist, a faithful teacher and expounder of God's Word, and as a powerful defender of the faith once delivered to the saints.

Meeting some people may not be a pleasant experience. Their outlook on life may make it a hardship rather than a pleasure. There are even some Christians and the words "uplifting and refreshing" do not readily come to mind when we contemplate seeing them.

However, Ian Paisley is not one of them. Even in the most difficult of times and under the most severe pressure he carries with him a faith in God and a love for Christ that encourages and inspires those with whom he meets.

The Bible declares "iron sharpeneth iron; so a man sharpeneth the countenance of his friend." Those of us who have worked closely with Ian Paisley can appreciate the truth of those words with regard to the manner in which all of our hearts have been encouraged and invigorated by his outgoing personality, his generosity of spirit, coupled with an infectious sense of humour and a genuine love for his fellow-man.

In the affairs of State God has seen fit to honour him, enabling him for many years to be a standard-bearer for law and order, truth and righteousness, and our civil and religious liberties. Only eternity will reveal the impact his witness for God has made on the spiritual and political life of our Province.

I salute him in the Lord and count it a privilege to know him as a friend and colleague.

Dr. Cooke ministered in our Mount Merrion, Belfast, Rasharkin, Co. Antrim and Armagh City Churches, and served until his retirement as Deputy Moderator of the Free Presbyterian Church and Professor of Homiletics in the Whitefield College of the Bible.

DR. FRANK McCLELLAND

It was one of those small providences that led to a major change for our family. Two farmers, Joe and John, after finishing their chores on an autumn day in 1948, were having a chat.

Joe, the younger of the two, had been at an Orange Order demonstration, and was telling John about what he saw and heard. At the parade rendezvous a flat-bed truck served as a platform for the speakers to address the Orangemen.

On the platform were several suave, accomplished ministers. But Joe's attention was drawn to "a tall thin youth wearing a clerical collar". Joe decided to stop and listen. He wondered what this raw youth would have to say.

Joe was astonished at the eloquence and power of delivery of the twenty-two year old preacher. He said to John, "you like good preaching. You should find out where he preaches - I think his name is Paisley."

John, my step-father, checked the newspaper Church ads and found that the Rev Paisley's church, Ravenhill Evangelical Mission Church, was on the Ravenhill Road in Belfast, only about three miles from our farm home.

The next Sunday we were driven in our little Morris 8 to the church in Belfast. I was not greatly interested. Our family belonged to a country church where, for me as a twelve year old boy, the most interesting thing was to guess at what stage one of the leading elders fell asleep. He always did - and little wonder, for the droning of the uninspired clergyman would send anyone to the land of nod.

Deadness pervaded the whole service and the minister obviously knew little experimentally of God's grace.

The Psalms, which I now love, were sung mournfully. Christian joy was noticeable by its absence. It was always a relief to me when the caretaker arose and left the Meeting House - a sure sign the service was about to end.

The church was completely surrounded by a graveyard and at that time its deadness seemed to permeate the whole church.

What a complete change we experienced on that first Sunday in Ravenhill. The Church was well filled with ordinary people who seemed to be genuinely happy as they anticipated the start of the service. We watched, fascinated, as the young preacher made his way to the pulpit.

His face was younger than his twenty-two years. He smiled radiantly. My mother remarked to me afterwards that his joy seemed to come from an inner peace he possessed. At that time I thought Christians were supposed to look miserable as a badge of their superior piety. Sadly, there are still many of that ilk abroad today.

There was no choir in Ravenhill, no precentor, no drab singing. The young preacher led the singing with great vigour and a booming voice - not always in tune - but he and the congregation made a joyful and happy sound as together they praised the Lord.

The opening prayer was something I had never encountered before. Here was a young man who prayed as if he meant it and also believed that God would answer his petitions.

A series of fervent 'Amens' punctuated each prayer petition - something totally unknown in our previous church.

It was the sermon, however, that made the biggest impact on our family. Never had we in Church been subjected to the sonic assault on our eardrums as we had that day.

The booming quality of the preacher's voice, the obvious sincerity of his delivery, the power of his exposition, the living presentation of the Word of God, the presence of God in the service, all combined to make a tremendous impact on our family. We never went back to our original church again.

As a family we were in Ravenhill when the Free Presbyterian Church of Ulster was born in adversity in 1951. Several of our family members came to Christ through the faithful preaching at Ravenhill.

My stepfather became a founding elder in the Sandown Road congregation and served the Lord faithfully until his death in May 1972. My brother came to Christ through Dr Paisley's preaching and served as minister in our Sandown Road, Mourne and Londonderry congregations.

In 1969, while my wife and I were living in the United States, the minister of the church we attended was murdered and I was a witness of the crime. Subsequently, I was led by the Lord to return to Ulster and called by God to preach. I served for seven years as minister of Tandragee Free Presbyterian Church, until the Lord broke the provincial mould in 1976 and led me to Toronto to start the first Free Presbyterian Church outside of Ireland. A thriving multi-national Church and School in Toronto bears testimony to the Lord's hand upon the Free Presbyterian Church.

Our family has much cause to rejoice because of that simple chat by two farmers in 1948. That providential meeting has been multiplied thousands of times throughout the world. In Ireland, North and South, Scotland, Wales, England, Germany, Australia, the United States and Canada, grateful Christians thank the Lord for saving grace, sustaining power and solid preaching. To them there is no argument. God brought the Free Presbyterian Church into being for "such a time as this".

THE CARRYDUFF MISSION

In the late fifties I, and a number of other young Christians, started a Youth Fellowship in "Murphy's Loft".

As its name suggests it was an upper room above the garage behind the home of Sydney Murphy in Carryduff, County Down. It became the scene of a remarkable Gospel mission in 1960.

The room could seat about 50 or 60 people, where, each Sunday evening, Mr Murphy held an after-church service. The Youth Fellowship met each Saturday evening.

I had felt for some time that a Mission with Dr Paisley would be a thing to be prayed for, but was not sure how to broach the subject with Mr Murphy, who was a respected member of the local Baptist Church.

I need not have worried, however, for the Lord answered prayer in a remarkable way. Mr Murphy came to me one night and suggested that the young people should organise a Gospel Mission with - Dr Paisley as preacher!

That Mission was held in 1960, lasted for five weeks, and God wonderfully moved. Many souls were saved, backsliders restored and God's people revived. It was as if God drew back the curtain a little and gave us a small taste of what genuine revival is like.

A unique feature of the Mission was the Prayer Meetings, where the presence of the Lord was real and palpable. One the Saturday night before the Mission started, what was to be a half-hour of prayer starting at 9.00pm continued until 1.00am on the Sunday morning. Young people were crying to God mightily and God was answering.

There were some unique characters who came along and joined with the young people. One used to pray each night that God would give her a smile of her face. She did not ask to be made like Moses or Stephen, but "like Cherry Blossom shoe polish!"

One dear lady used to roam all over the Bible in her prayers. Dr Paisley would respond, "You're in Jeremiah now, sister, that's Daniel now," and so on.

The joy of the Lord pervaded the atmosphere and the power of the Lord was manifested in the prayer meetings and the lasting results of the mission.

I have locked in my memory forever the sight of my brother James, dressed in a brown suit, going into the inquiry room after one service.

We could never get him to come to the Ravenhill Church with us, but because the mission was close to home he could hardly refuse the invitation. We had long prayed for him and what a thrill it was that night God answered prayer and saved him. He was called into the ministry soon after.

That Mission was undoubtedly directed by the Lord. Most of those young people grew up and are still serving the Lord faithfully today - many now grandmothers and grandfathers!

It has been our continual desire and prayer that the curtain drawn back a little in 1960 would some day be fully opened to reveal a gracious and glorious spiritual awakening in Ulster, and wherever God's Word is faithfully preached.

Dr. Frank McClelland is Minister of Toronto Free Presbyterian Church.

REV. JAMES BEGGS

In 1951, the year under God of the constitution of the Free Presbyterian Church of Ulster, I was a young teenager of just 16 years of age, the son of a staunch Presbyterian family in the County of Tyrone. When the news filtered through that there was some disruption in the Presbyterian church in Crossgar and that a young man named Ian Paisley was at the centre of the storm it meant very little to me in my carefree boyhood days. I was yet in my sins without Christ and received the news with something like indignation that this firebrand Paisley should upset the status quo of my beloved Presbyterian establishment. I was yet to be taught the truth of the whole affair but not before my darkened mind was enlightened, my will renewed and the whole religious prejudice of my heart broken by the grace of God. Little did I know that under the mysterious Providence of God I was to become closely identified, not only with the Paisley family, but that God in His inscrutable will was to lead me by His grace into the ministry of the Free Presbyterian Church. But that is a story for another occasion. Suffice it is to say that I married Dr Paisley's sister Margaret in 1961 and that I was licensed as a minister of the church in 1966.

FOR SUCH A TIME AS THIS

As I near the end of my active pastorate in the ministry in Ballymena I can now trace the hand of God in all the affairs of this latter 20th Century, and have no doubt in my mind that God in His wisdom raised up Dr Ian Paisley and the Secession of the Free Presbyterian Church for such a time as this. In these 33 years of ministry and intimate fellowship with Ian Paisley there are many incidents that spring readily to mind which manifest the unique anointing that rests upon His faithful servant - none more so than the remarkable movement of God the Holy Ghost in what is now affectionately known amongst us as the '75 Mission.

For some years we had been praying towards a campaign of this nature for the town of Ballymena, and in answer to that prayer Dr Paisley approached us, having been spoken to by the Lord regarding a Gospel Campaign in Ballymena. It became abundantly clear to us that this was the will of God for us in regard to an evangelistic campaign. Dr Paisley was to be the Evangelist, Rev William McCrea the song leader and the Town Hall, Ballymena the venue. The date was set for 31st August, 1975 and the necessary organisation was put in motion. Prayer was intensified and over the summer months many special prayer meetings were conducted. The evident burden of these meetings was that God would visit His people and that Ballymena might be touched with the power of God in salvation. We were convinced however that *"Except the Lord build the house they labour in vain that build it."* God's people agonised for souls and sought the Lord for the enduement of power for His servants. At 6.00am on the first Sunday morning of the campaign a number of God's people met for earnest prayer. The Lord gave us the assurance in our hearts that He was going to work but none of us was prepared for what was about to happen. We were given a special promise from the Lord which we preached on in the Sunday morning service. Mal. 3:10 *"there shall not be room enough to receive it"*. That very afternoon God was to prove His promise to us in a way, despite our earnest praying, that we did not really expect. Dr Paisley preached the opening message with particular compassion and power, Mr McCrea sang with great blessing, but when under the appeal 20-30 people came out in response we were totally unprepared for it. Indeed it was true there was not enough room to receive it. No counsellors had been arranged, not enough room had been allocated for enquirers and our unbelief had been sorely exposed despite our many prayers. How good God is to bless us even in our foolish unbelieving state. He blesses us in spite of ourselves. That afternoon of power was to set the scene for all the nights of the mission to follow. There was not a single night but souls were saved, until by the final service 351 precious souls had passed through the enquiry rooms. How evident it was that God's servant had been sent to Ballymena for such a time as this.

The following three nights were, I believe, to be the fulcrum around which the blessing of the mission was to revolve. On these nights Dr Paisley came with a burden on his heart for the people of God. Those messages from God smote our hearts with conviction and power and we cried to God for mercy and pardon. The Word of God set His people praying and what prayer God gave His children. On three mornings each week forty to fifty people gathered to pray and cry to God for souls. Before the service the people queued to get in to the prayer times. Many testified that all day they had anticipated with joy the times of prayer. Those who had already prayed audibly, vacated their seats that others might be accommodated and our good and gracious God sent down his power upon us. The late night prayer meetings were particularly memorable. They were not for those of a timorous nature. The whole street knew there was a prayer meeting on and some of the prayers were somewhat unorthodox, for the young converts were already mingling with us in prayer. Things happened that no doubt would have been frowned upon in certain circles or in a less spiritual atmosphere, but there was every evidence that God was with us and that His servants were preaching, singing and praying under the mighty anointing of God.

And notable things were already happening. Men who had long prayed for their families saw them united in grace. Deep conviction of sin characterised the converts. Godly sorrow for sin was in evidence as night after night sinners wept their way to the cross. One strapping young man came out one night in the appeal and as I accompanied him up the stairs he staggered as if he was punch drunk. I sat him down and began to counsel him in the usual formal way and immediately he gripped my arm, crying out in brokenness, "Mr Beggs just lead me to Christ! Just lead me to Christ" So I simply led him to Christ and a great calm came over his soul.

The culmination of the mission may well have come when two close friends and loyal supporters of Dr Paisley walked the aisle for God on the same night. John McDowell and Roy Gillespie had been the object of many prayers. Others were struck off the prayer list for souls but John and Roy remained until that night when God smote them with saving power and united them in Christ.

In the end the mission was extended by two weeks over the original time planned. Who can ever forget the last Sunday evening or the scene when well over 40 souls were being counselled in the Minor Town Hall. The Lord had done great things for us whereof we were glad.

During the next 18 months almost 100 people were received into the Communicant membership of the church. Some of them are members of our Session and Committee and others Sunday School teachers.

As we face the new millennium there is no doubt that we need such a move of God in power by His Holy Spirit. The God who answers by fire is still alive. May God send us to our knees to seek His face again.

Rev. James Beggs is Minister of J. Kyle Paisley Memorial
Free Presbyterian Church, Ballymena.

REV. IVAN FOSTER

When the year 2000 dawns, irrespective of the significance of leaving the 1900s and beginning a new century and a new millennium, it will not supersede in my heart the events of the 1960s as the most momentous in my life.

It was then that I was saved. It was then that I experienced the power of the Holy Ghost. It was then that I became a member of Dr Paisley's congregation. It was then that I entered the ministry of the Free Presbyterian Church. It was then too that I spent three months in prison in company with Dr Paisley, a man who has had an influence for good upon the lives of many, many people here in Ulster and across the world.

That was a most momentous period in the history of our denomination.

On July 23rd, 1966, when my three-month stay in Crumlin Road Prison began, I was already well acquainted with Dr Paisley. I had also been a student for the ministry for eighteen months. The prison sentence, was the result of an attempt by ecumenical clerics and politicians to silence the growing witness of our church against the beginnings of the betrayal to ecclesiastical and political Romanism. I had been a member of Ravenhill Free Presbyterian Church for two years, having been converted on April 5th, 1964, and had been in attendance at this church since April 12th. My first Sabbath evening as a Christian was spent listening enraptured to God's Word being preached, in a fashion I had never heard before, nor, I must add, have ever heard since.

The Free Presbyterian Church was very much a family affair then. Everyone knew everyone else. Student ministers, being rather thin on the ground, were treated as sons, grandsons, nephews. What love was showered on our unworthy heads! An essential element of my training was acting as Dr Paisley's assistant. What an experience that was!

By July 1966, I was therefore on familiar though respectful terms with the Moderator. However, the three months in prison lifted my acquaintance with Dr Paisley to a higher plane.

During the three months, in the many quiet hours we spent there, (John Wylie was there as well,) we were permitted to share in our cells, I benefited greatly from his spiritual analysis of the situation in Ulster, and his understanding of the working of the spirit of apostasy, and the havoc that it must invariably bring about, has followed me throughout my ministry. I learned to dread the apostasy taking place within Ulster's main denominations then for the evil and hellish thing that it was. I still do and cannot lightly look on its activities all around us. The insight granted to me in my prison cell classroom lives on in my soul.

I also benefited from Dr Paisley's maturity as a Christian warrior.

I had spent the first night of my sentence in the police cells, being arrested after the time Crumlin Road Jail received inmates. Consequently, I spent my first night amongst the "smokers, bokers and chokers" who found a lodging place there virtually each night! Believe me, that night lives on in my memory too!

When we met up with Dr Paisley and John Wylie the next day, I was right glad to do so. We naturally talked about what lay ahead of us for this was a new experience for us all. Dr Paisley mentioned how he had prayed that the Lord would give him favour with the jailer as He had done for Joseph (Gen. 39:21). I can clearly still remember my sense of my own spiritual adolescence and thinking of how good it must be to have such a ready acquaintance with the experiences of the saints of God whose lives are recorded in God's Word, so that such timely thoughts occur to you.

I also observed, and I hope I learned from it also, the utter dedication of the man to the cause of Christ. For him, the whole episode of the imprisonment was viewed only in the light of its impact upon God's work. The consequences for him personally or for his family did not dominate his thinking. Naturally, he had concerns but they were submerged beneath anxiety for the witness of Christ in the land and the opportunity granted to the people to see where ecumenism was taking them.

From the moment the imprisonment began, the Lord was pleased to stir up a tremendous interest and sense of alarm amongst both Christians and unbelievers. Meetings conducted by our brethren, Revs Bert Cooke, John Douglas, Alan Cairns, William Beattie and others, were usually convened at the request of people outside the Free Presbyterian Church. Multitudes attended those meetings. They took place in Orange halls and at crossroads, in fields and in town halls, and multitudes attended to hear these men preach God's Word and expound it, showing the relevance of the political and religious events then taking place.

The Government of the day, under Terence O'Neill, only added to the interest by outlawing gatherings of three or more people within a radius of seven miles from Belfast's city centre. That tended to heighten the sense of alarm felt by Protestants and drove the meetings out into the countryside where the bulk of non-conformity was to be found.

These were times of a hunger for God's Word and what it had to say on the events taking place. Poor Dr Paisley! Having laboured from the beginning of his ministry back in 1946 to bring about such a day, he was incarcerated in jail when it dawned! He was ready to scale the 25-foot high walls to get out and get at the preaching.

Perhaps the chief benefit obtained from my three months of "close fellowship" with Dr Paisley was in the seasons of prayer we all shared together. Each day there was a combined time of prayer in John Wylie's cell, it being between the other two. What times of waiting on God those were! Now, 33 years after, I realise what a privilege it was for a 22-year-old student minister to share in such fellowship. Those times left a mark on my soul and on my life.

A very important element of my prison experience were the times of happy conversation. In three months you may hear an awful lot of reminiscence and story-telling. I drank in the accounts of the events of the previous fifteen years of the Free Presbyterian Church's existence from the lips of the man who was ever at the centre of those times.

In writing about those three months, my soul has been stirred and blessed afresh as the happy memories rise up in my mind. Yes, a new century is about to dawn. A new millennium is about to commence. But I will let others get excited at their approach and ring the bells to welcome them.

As for me, I will hold on to 1966 with gladness and with thanks to God for the mercies enjoyed then.

I do wish and pray for the next generation that they will encounter in the new century something of the blessing that was poured forth some 33 years ago, only in an even greater measure.

Rev. Ivan Foster is the Minister of Kilskeery
Free Presbyterian Church.

REV. WILLIAM BEATTIE

"For if thou altogether holdest thy peace at this time, then shall there enlargement and deliverence arise to the Jews from another place; but thou and thy father's house shall be destroyed: and who knoweth whether thou art come to the kingdom for such a time as this?" This text, Esther 4:14, which is the title of this book, aptly sums up the central role of Dr Ian RK Paisley MP MEP as God's man with God's message, with a powerful anointing upon him in the unfolding catastrophe both spiritual and political in Northern Ireland. As in Esther's day, God has provided a champion for His cause and His people.

My relationship with Dr Paisley goes back to my childhood when he and my father were already the closest of friends. To my father, and later to myself, Dr Paisley was someone special raised up of God. My father died in January 1963 and when Dr Paisley called at our home he quoted the words of the prophet Isaiah *"The righteous perisheth, and no man layeth it to heart: none considering that the righteous is taken away from the evil to come"* Isaiah 57:1.

"The evil to come" was manifested almost immediately in April 1963 when Captain Terence O'Neill became the Prime Minister of Northern Ireland. The local Ecumenical Movement, already a force for evil, was gathering momentum in Northern Ireland. Following the New Delhi Assembly of the World Council of Churches in 1961, it had found a political ally to forward its ecclesiastical objectives in the political realm. By 1965, O'Neill, in a vain attempt to appease Republicanism, invited Sean Lemass and later Jack Lynch as Irish Prime Ministers to visit Northern Ireland.

Dr Paisley, who as Moderator of the Free Presbyterian Church of Ulster, had been established by God as the champion for Christ contending for the Faith in the battle against apostasy and modernism in the major denominations, all of which had become fervently ecumenical, now rallied the Protestants of Ulster against the joint forces of apostasy and appeasement in Church and State. Protest marches and rallies were organised and hundreds and then thousands gathered in support of powerful meetings in the halls and fields and town centres throughout the Province. The issues were addressed, the Word of God was preached, hearts were stirred, the gospel was proclaimed, and souls were converted. The opposition in the media, in the pulpits and in Parliament was diabolical, but God honoured His servant by working powerfully in mercy and many souls were redeemed.

Dr Paisley's bold and courageous stand against the twin evils of Ecumenism and O'Neillism was being honoured of God in an amazing demonstration of the Holy Spirit's power. It was a God-given privilege of unspeakable magnitude for me to share a little in the experience as I accompanied him and participated on many occasions as a student minister of the Free Presbyterian Church of Ulster. At that time, under his leadership, my own ministry developed in prayer, in preaching and in dealing with the issues facing us today.

In June 1966 another stage in the "evil to come" unfolded when Dr Paisley led a protest march to the General Assembly of the Irish Presbyterian Church. The march was attacked by Republicans as it passed by the Belfast Markets and then it was stopped by the RUC to allow the ecumenical procession of guests of the Assembly to cross Howard Street to the Assembly Building. The peaceful protest was the most powerful to date with a multitude of supporters participating.

The day following the protest O'Neill sent his Minister of Home Affairs, Mr Brian McConnell, to assure the Irish Presbyterians that such a protest would not occur again.

Following that assurance charges were brought against Dr Paisley, Rev John Wylie and Rev Ivan Foster who, being found guilty in the court, refused to be bound over to keep the peace and were subsequently jailed for three months. To sign the bond to keep the peace would have been an acceptance of guilt when there was none.

God honoured the three brethren and throughout the early autumn, during their imprisonment, thousands were reached with the gospel and converted to Christ at protest rallies and parades throughout Northern Ireland and in the regular services in our churches. New congregations were established and many more were to follow over the years in Northern Ireland, in the United Kingdom mainland, in the North American continent and in Australia. Formation of new congregations continues as Dr Paisley leads us with the same unique spiritual dynamism as before.

In 1968 Brian McConnell resigned and was replaced in the Stormont South Antrim constituency by Richard Ferguson who, when he was elected, gave support to O'Neill's programme of appeasement in breach of an understanding that he would not do so. By 1969 Dr Paisley's campaign against O'Neill had gained such momentum that O'Neill called a General Election.

Dr Paisley and I, with Rev John Wylie and others, stood as Protestant Unionists in opposition to O'Neill's policies. The vote for Dr Paisley and myself was such that one year later O'Neill and Ferguson resigned and at the subsequent by-elections in 1970 Dr Paisley was elected to represent Bannside and I was elected to represent South Antrim. As we took our seats in Parliament the Lord had worked a wondrous thing in that Dr Paisley had replaced Terence O'Neill and I had taken Brian McConnell's seat. The God of Esther who had replaced Haman with Mordecai had replaced the Prime Minister and the Minister of Home Affairs in the Stormont Parliament and their seats in Parliament were now occupied by Dr Paisley and myself! Those who had vowed to use their power to stop the opposition of the Free Presbyterian Church to the ecumenical movement had been removed from office and had been replaced by the Moderator of the Free Presbyterian Church and one of its ministers.

To the Lord we give all the glory. It was the Lord who blessed Dr Paisley's leadership with a breath of revival at rallies, in gospel campaigns and in personal evangelism. We all shared and participated in that revival.

As the Ravenhill congregation expanded on the Ravenhill Road the Ulster Hall became the venue for thousands until the opening of the Martyrs Memorial Church in 1969. I recall those days of excitement and joy in the midst of fierce opposition from the establishment in Church and State with humble thanksgiving to God for the man whom God gave to us in our time of need. For us, God had chosen someone whom the world considered to be foolish, to confound their Satanic wisdom that no flesh should glory but that the glory would be the Lord's.

The ensuing terror and turmoil in Ulster, the loss of and maiming of thousands of innocent lives, as well as the widespread mayhem that followed in the joint wake of O'Neillism and Ecumenism over the past thirty years and more, along with the present malignant growth of Romanism and Republicanism, which is the inevitable fruit of that unholy alliance, has more than vindicated under God the call and ministry of Dr Paisley. The mantle of the Lord has been upon him in a special way. He has come to the kingdom *"for such a time as this"*.

It has been and continues to be a blessing to serve our Saviour alongside the most outstanding servant of God this century, and it is my heart's desire that he might be long spared to continue for the sake of our Lord Jesus Christ and His Bride the Church.

Rev. William J Beattie is the Minister of Dunmurry
Free Presbyterian Church.

REV. STANLEY BARNES

Charles Kingsley, a famous preacher of a former generation was asked on one occasion what was the secret of his successful ministry. His reply was somewhat simple and yet significant, "I had a friend."

Many of us feel exactly the same sentiment as that preacher. We look back and thank God our lives have been touched by the ministry and friendship of Dr. I. R. K Paisley M.P. M.E.P.

My first personal recollections of him can be traced back to 1959, the year that marked the centenary of the great 1859 Revival which swept across Ulster. It was also the year of my conversion to Jesus Christ. At that time Dr. Paisley was becoming a household name in Ulster as a result of his great evangelistic missions and increasing involvement in religious controversies. One evening, after I attended a prayer meeting in the old Ravenhill Free Presbyterian Church, I decided to apply for membership of the church. I became a Free Presbyterian.

Some months later, at a Sunday morning service, God spoke to me in an unmistakable manner. Dr. Paisley was preaching on the text, "The children of Ephraim being armed, turned back in the day of battle." During the course of his sermon he said, "Perhaps there is a young man here this morning whom God is calling to the battle, but alas He will have to write across the pages of your life, 'You turned back in the day of battle.'" Through His servant that morning I knew that God was calling me into His service. I am glad I found grace to obey the call of God.

Soon afterwards I told an old aunt who belonged to the Plymouth Brethren, what had taken place in my life. Her reply was an exclamation, "O dear! You will never be out of trouble with that man!" Little did I know how prophetic her words were!

Having known Dr. Paisley as a pastor, college lecturer and Moderator of the Free Presbyterian Presbytery, I have found life to have been anything but dull during these past thirty-three years.

As a pastor, Dr. Paisley has a shepherd's heart for his flock and can weep with those that weep and rejoice with those that rejoice. Charles E. Jefferson wrote in his book,"The Minister as a Shepherd,""A shepherd cannot shine. He cannot cut a figure. His work must be done in obscurity... His work calls for continuous self effacement. It is a form of service which eats up a man's life. It makes a man old before his time. Every good shepherd lays down his life for the sheep. It is the weakling and not the giants who neglect their people."

As a student it was an unforgettable experience to attend Dr. Paisley's lectures when he was Professor of Church History at the Free Presbyterian Theological Hall. His love for the Reformation and the great spiritual revivals of former years was very much in evidence as he lectured to us. The Presbyterian missionary leader, Dr. A. T. Pearson used to say that"history is His Story." Dr. Paisley holds that same conviction. His study and knowledge of Church History has been an inspiration to all his students.

As Moderator of the Free Presbyterian Church, his leadership has been invaluable. I believe this powerful leadership is one of the reasons our denomination has witnessed such phenomenal growth throughout the world. Other denominations have been formed in Ulster since the turn of the twentieth century, but none of them have witnessed the same growth as the Free Presbyterian Church. I am convinced that the lack of strong leadership in these churches was the main contributing factor why they did not experience similar growth. Great spiritual movements in the past have been spear-headed by men like Dr. Paisley who were"brought to the kingdom for such a time as this."

For me it has been a great privilege to share in the ministry of the Martyrs Memorial Free Presbyterian Church for many years. I have had special involvement at the Wednesday night prayer meetings when Dr. Paisley has been out of the country either preaching or on parliamentary business. I recall on one occasion he asked me to conduct the midweek prayer meeting. Much to my surprise he arrived at the church just before the service began. He informed me that he was just going to commence the service, say a few words and then leave me to preach. He then said,"Let's have a word of prayer." The clerk of session Mr. W. P. Moore and myself stood by while Dr. Paisley prayed, "Lord I thank you I am not a goat but one of your sheep. When you put your sheep forth you go before them. Go before us. Bless these other fellows. I am not sure if they are sheep or goats, but bless them anyway. Amen." How could we add our"Amen" to such a prayer?

Dr. Paisley's love for books is well known to all who are acquainted with him. His good friend from Virginia Beach, USA, Dr. Rod Bell, once commented to me,"To go on a holiday with Dr. Paisley involves visiting all the graveyards and second-hand bookshops in the area."

As students he advised us"not to waste time on reading chaff when you can read the wheat." I remember telling him on one occasion about a minister who had recently died, and that I had been able to obtain some good books from his library. "Is there anything worthwhile left?" he enquired. I told him that there was still a shelf of books on the Quakers."Quakers!" he exclaimed, bursting into laughter, "I have enough quakers around me without reading about them."

Personally, I have found Dr. Paisley to be a faithful servant of Jesus Christ who has had a greater influence on my life and ministry than any other man I have ever known. Solomon reminds us that "A friend loveth at all times, and a brother is born for adversity." Proverbs 17 v.17.

There is nothing like the university of adversity to help make us appreciate just who are our true friends. I thank God that I too can say, like Charles Kingsley, "I had a friend."

Rev Stanley Barnes is the Minister of Hillsborough
Free Presbyterian Church.

REV. DAVID McILVEEN

God in His gracious providence is pleased to convey His will through men and women who have fully submitted their hearts to His glorious purpose.

Every generation has been honoured by such God-appointed servants, whose leadership qualities have been divinely gifted to the church. For while God in His sovereignty could work without the use of the human instrument He has revealed to the world that "it pleaseth Him through the foolishness of preaching to save them that believe."

Few could argue that Dr Paisley has not been God's man for such a time as this. For more than five decades the mighty forces of evil have, like the raging billows, crashed daily upon a ministry that has stood the test, and is presented by God as a testimony of His favour to multitudes of people.

Blessed with an exceedingly tender spirit and with a sympathetic understanding of peoples' needs, Dr Paisley's love for the Saviour, love for the Scripture and love for the Saints, provide the major elements for one raised up by God.

Such devotion demands a forfeiting of personal gain and a sacrificing of personal popularity, so that the cause of Christ's kingdom might be the constant priority in the instrument that God is pleased to use. To seek the approval of the world would render such a vessel unclean. The world's acclaim and adoration cannot sit comfortably with the Lord's blessing, a blessing which Dr Paisley has freely shared with many throughout his public ministry. On several occasions I have been privileged to stand with him, in what can only be described as "once-in-a-life time" experiences. My personal recollections of the protest against the Pope's visit to the European Parliament in Strasbourg remains to this day a most vivid testimony of one whose desire is to glorify God and to enjoy Him for ever.

The seasons of prayer that we had prior to the day of the protest were especially sweet to the soul. The Lord Himself drew near with a gracious sense of His presence that instilled confidence into our hearts. A great peace descended over our fellowship as we walked around the centre of the city the evening before the Pope's visit. I had already been told that my admittance to the Parliament the next day depended upon my acceptance of not getting involved in the public protest, a demand that was reluctantly agreed to. However this turned out to be advantageous as I was allowed a seat in the part of the public gallery where the MEP's guests were sitting. Early the next day we made our way to the Parliament where the security was already in evidence. Immediately after breakfast we went down to Dr Paisley's office which was turned into a "little sanctuary". Periodically throughout the morning we had times of prayer as together we contemplated before the Lord the enormity of the challenge facing the Lord's servant.

As the time for the Pope's arrival drew near, Dr Paisley urged me to go and take my place in the chamber. My seat was right beside the wife of the President of the Parliament. Taking my seat, I looked over towards the President's chair, where he and his officials were already in position. Then I heard his wife say to the lady next to her, "I hope Paisley will do nothing silly today". I smiled inwardly at her comment knowing that he along with many millions throughout the world, was about to witness one of the greatest protests since the reformation.

Momentarily I glanced in the direction of Dr Paisley, and when I looked behind the President's chair I saw the Pope about to make his entrance into the chamber. To me he appeared nervous as he slowly turned around to his escorts, and as he made his way into the chamber the people rose to clap the man of sin and the son of perdition, that is, all but two people.

As the clapping subsided there was a moment of silence and then the booming voice of Dr Paisley rang throughout the building. His denunciation against the Pope brought immediate acts of violence against Dr Paisley as surrounding members sought to silence the Lord's servant. I watched somewhat horrified from the gallery as Dr Paisley was dragged from his seat. Immediately I made my way to the main doors of the chamber, passing a security guard who asked me why I was leaving before the Pope had started to speak.

Dr Paisley, although hurt as a result of the incident, was surrounded by the world's media. The details of the protest were transmitted throughout the world giving much encouragement to God's people, and reminding the ecumenical church that God had not left Himself without a witness.

I was also privileged to go to Rome and protest on the street with Dr Paisley at the visit of the Archbishop of Canterbury to the Pope.

Together we have travelled many miles, discussed many portions of scriptures, witnessed many wonderful happenings, especially in Africa and shared in sweet fellowship with the Lord. Of such a man called to the kingdom for such a time as this, I can truly say, as the King of Syria said of Elisha, "the man of God has come hither."

Rev. McIlveen is the Minister of Sandown
Free Presbyterian Church, Belfast

MRS. EILEEN PAISLEY

Recently my husband and I celebrated our forty-third wedding anniversary. That morning my husband said to me, "Where have all the years gone?" For once I had no answer. It seemed that we had just blinked a few times and the years had melted away. Then we began to recount the blessings that our loving Heavenly Father had poured out upon us during those years and indeed throughout both our lives, and we said with the Psalmist, "Thy mercies are new every morning."

Looking back over my life I can rejoice that I had Godly parents who not only read God's Book to us but practised its teachings in their daily lives and laid good foundations for their children to build upon. They taught us the preciousness of time and the sinfulness of wasting time. I find myself still benefiting from their wise counsel. I shall be eternally indebted to my older brother who came to Christ early in his life and prayed for me. He took me to the gospel mission where I came to Christ. During my husband's imprisonments my sister came and stayed with me, and I could not count the times my younger brother baby-sat for our children. These are blessings and kindnesses which all too often are overlooked, but which I can never forget.

In Psalm 31 verse 15 we read, "My times are in thy hand," and it is wonderful what God does for us when we leave our lives in His hand. He leads us and overrules all things to His own glory. The psalmist makes no mistake when this verse continues, "deliver me from the hand of mine enemies, and from them that persecute me." How often my husband and I have prayed that prayer during our marriage and indeed before it!

Ian and I met in 1950 under unusual circumstances. When I was at school I was interested in going into nursing but I changed my mind and I found myself going to Business College which I really enjoyed and when I completed my studies I obtained a situation as junior secretary. My father and brother were members of the National Union of Protestants and I used to attend with them the great rallies in the YMCA. When special visiting preachers would come to address these rallies I took down their messages in short-hand, and these were then printed in the NUP's magazine.

Now, the honorary treasurer of the NUP was none other than the young minister of Ravenhill Evangelical Mission Church. I often saw him sitting with the others on the platform, but was too busy to pay attention to anyone or anything except the job in hand. One day, however, I had to go to the NUP office in Howard Street, and who should come in but you know who. We spoke briefly to one another, and when I had completed my errand I left.

Some weeks later I received a telephone call to my office. The voice at the other end was saying, "Miss Cassells, would you go somewhere with me?" Jokingly I replied, "O certainly sir, sure I'd go anywhere with you. Who are you anyway?"

A great peal of laughed tumbled down the telephone, and he explained, "It's Ian Paisley. I'm starting a magazine of my own, and I wondered if you would come to a meeting and take down my sermon in shorthand so that I could have it printed?" That magazine was the Revivalist, which started life as an "independent voice" but after the foundation of the Free Presbyterian Church became its official magazine. I am still proof reading its pages.

That was the beginning of our friendship, a friendship which very soon blossomed into a deep, strong love which has passed the test of time, and a lot of other tests as well.

Due to circumstances beyond our control, we had to wait until 1956 before we could get married, so we both learned the art of patience. These circumstances all began with the letter 'M' - the church was Manseless, Moneyless and the committee was characterised by Meanness. If they had all been ghosts they wouldn't have given the minister a fright between them!

But God had it all planned out for us.

Just after we met Ian conducted a gospel mission in his father's church in Ballymena. The church was packed to overflowing and the meetings had moved to the Town Hall. It too was packed, and best of all over four hundred souls came to Christ. At that mission I learned to do enquiry room work and had the joy of dealing with many young people.

A mission was planned for February 1951 in Crossgar. Much prayer and preparation had gone into that mission, and when we arrived on the Saturday evening for the opening meeting, the doors of the Church Hall were locked! The Down Presbytery had met that afternoon and decided that no mission would take place. It was a very wet evening, but despite the weather the elders and the people decided to have a march of witness around the town, and they then proceeded to a little mission hall which was hastily and willingly given so that the mission could be held.

It was a wonderful mission and God abundantly blessed the preaching of His Word. A great number of people came to Christ, some very notorious sinners amongst them.

Most of the elders and committee of that church in Crossgar resigned and after a prolonged time of prayer seeking God's will, it was decided to commence a new work, separated from a growing apostasy.

Of course there was a lot of hassle after the Free Presbyterian Church came into being. Many of those who joined with us suffered various forms of persecution, and indeed to this day we are discriminated against by certain people and certain organisations. People with whom we had had friendly relations no longer counted us among their friends. Invitations to conduct missions were cancelled and organisations of which my husband had been a member now expelled him.

Nevertheless, God was with him, and also with me. He led us in ways we knew not. Those years of waiting were times of preparation, of learning to keep calm, learning that God's timing is always best, and learning to "endure hardness as good soldiers of Jesus Christ". We both learnt the value of time, and the quality of time. When Ian was away on missions, sometimes we didn't see each other for weeks at a time. If I complained my mother used to console me by telling me that during the war years girls didn't see their boyfriends for years, never mind weeks!

I also learned that keeping my mind and my hands occupied helped to shorten the time, and that was a worthwhile lesson. Back in the '50s not many people had the luxury of a telephone in their home, so the postman was a person of great importance. I looked forward to his daily visits and would eagerly flip through the mail, looking for the neat handwriting I knew so well!

During those years I met many people across Ulster at the various missions Ian conducted, and especially where new churches were springing up, and these people became lifetime friends with whom I still enjoy sweet fellowship.

The first thing we did when we got married was to set up a family altar in our home. That altar has remained strong through all the vicissitudes of our life and as our children came along they too learned to hallow the times we spent together in reading the Word of God and in praying . Someone has said "The family that prays together stays together", and we as a family have proved the truth of those words. Although four of our five children are married and have homes and families of their own, we all remain united in our love for God and His Word and in our love for one another. These times are most precious to us all.

God gave to us three daughters and twin sons, in that order, and early in their lives, each of them came to Christ. I had the joy of pointing three of them, Sharon, Cherith and Ian,to the Saviour. My husband led Kyle to Christ, and Rhonda was saved at a mission conducted by Drs. Bob Wells and Holland London, in the Ulster Hall, Belfast. We count ourselves to be millionaires, for we have riches more than all the gold in the world could buy. Who can put a price on the souls of our children?

I would give thanks to God for the partners He has given to the four of our children who are married. Our two sons-in-law, John and Andrew, are as precious to us as our own sons and our two daughters-in-law, Fiona and Janice, are patient and long-suffering wives whose husbands, like their father, are always busy, one in politics and one in preaching, and we love them all dearly.

Rhonda who still lives with us at home and is a source of great joy to us. There is never a dull moment when she is around. Her only complaint is that her parents are rebellious and difficult to manage! Her wit and humour are infectious and she is greatly loved by all her nieces and nephew.

Now that we have become grandparents and our family has increased, our joys have also increased, and even more so as one by one the four eldest, Lydia, Shane, Kara and Emily, have received Christ as their Saviour. We pray that when the three youngest, Danielle, Lucy and Bethany, come to understand God's simple plan of salvation, they too will put their trust in Him who said, 'Suffer the little children to come unto Me, and forbid them not, for of such is the kingdom of Heaven'.

My mother used to say to me, 'There is one sin Ian Paisley will never have to answer for, and that is the sin of wasting time'. And that is true. His life has been one of full-time service for God and his fellow-man, no matter the cost to himself or his family. Only the wife and family of a truly dedicated servant of God and minister of the gospel know the hours spent in prayer and meditation, reading and studying that go into the preparation of the messages he delivers. Some folk have the idea that a minister lifts his Bible, and then 'lifts' a sermon from some old dusty tome lying in his study, touches it up a little the way a photographer would do with an old photograph, then presents it to his congregation on Sunday. I have no doubt that some ministers do just that, but they are not true ministers of Jesus Christ.

How often have I wakened during the night to find the study light burning, and my husband sitting with bowed head at his desk, his face wet with tears, as he wrestled and agonized over the souls of his people. How lightly some people receive the word of God, and how quickly it evaporates from their carnal minds! How ungrateful, and what short memories some people have. The minister feeds them the finest of God's wheat, yet at the first opportunity that comes their way they hurl their fiery darts at him. Yes, we expect to be attacked by the Devil's crowd and we can defend ourselves against such attacks by 'putting on the whole armour of God', but we can be caught off-guard by our so-called friends, especially those for whom you have laboured in word and deed. Believe me, the wounds caused by their darts, either verbal or written, go deep into the heart, and are the hardest to heal. It is vital that early in our Christian life, and especially so for the Minister and his wife and family, to learn to 'endure hardness, as good soldiers of Jesus Christ', otherwise we would have long ago fallen in the battle.

During the course of our lives, my husband's duties have taken him all over the world, and that of course has meant separation for various periods of time. It is never easy to be separated, and one doesn't ever become 'used to it', but we have learnt to live with it and come to terms with it because it is God's work, and both of us have always endeavoured to put God first. That is something we have never regretted, for God is no one's debtor, and He has so blessed us, and given us far more abundantly than we could ever ask, and certainly far far more than we deserve.

But there are different kinds of separation; some are harder to bear than others. The hardest were the imprisonments, and although I could take the children each week to see their Dad, it was a heart-breaking experience for us all to be told that we couldn't kiss him or even touch him, and had to sit at one side of a long bare table while he sat at the other side with a warder beside him. How the iron went into the souls of my children, and how they suffered. I was too angry at the injustice of it all to even shed a tear, but I got rid of my frustrations by speaking at rallies all over Ulster. I remember the late Mr. James Nichol, our Clerk of Session at that time, coming to visit us at the old manse the night my husband was taken into prison. He was a most soft-hearted man, and he walked into the hall, put his arms around us, and burst into tears. I said, 'Mr. Nichol, don't cry or you'll make me cry too, and I'm far too angry to cry.' Our two eldest daughters, Sharon and Rhonda, were at school and other children taunted them by saying 'Your Daddy's just a jail-bird'. Now that is hard for young children to take, but they stood valiantly and stoutly defended their beloved Dad. Cherith was just 8 months old at her Dad's first imprisonment, and she fretted so much for him, and became so ill that I had to stop taking her on our weekly visits.

The separations when Ian travelled across the world to preach were difficult too, but in a different way. The longest and most arduous of these was during the building of the Martyrs Memorial Church. In order to raise funds for the building, Dr. Bob Jones Jr. organized a six-week programme of meetings for my husband across America. Those six weeks were spent on endless 'plane journeys, criss-crossing the USA and preaching every night. Each week my husband mailed several cheques home which were put in the building fund of the church. Many thousands of dollars were raised by my husband at that time. As well as that, all the cheques he received for television appearances, as well as fees for preaching around the country on Sunday afternoons or at after-church meetings,were given to the building fund. I think I can safely say that I do not know of any other minister in our denomination or in any other denomination who worked so hard to build a church, or whose family made such a sacrifice as did mine.

I can say truthfully that we suffered these separations joyfully for the furtherance of the gospel, and none of us regret anything we ever did, because we did it unto the Lord.

At the beginning of this article I said that God led Ian and me together in an unusual way. Our God is an unusual God. He has done unusual things for us, and blessed us in unusual ways. As we look towards the new millennium our trust is firmly in our unchangeable God, who has, I believe, brought us all to the kingdom for such a time as this, and Who will be our Guide, even beyond death. I am, I think justifiably, proud to be the wife of Ian Paisley.

Eileen Paisley.

He is tall and well built. He has very kind and smiling hazel eyes and wears glasses when reading or writing. His grey hair is neatly cut and well groomed. He is always neatly dressed in a suit with a matching shirt and bright tie. His shoes are always polished to a shine. In cold weather he wears a cap or Russian hat and gloves. His fingernails are well manicured and clean.

He is very generous and always carries a black leather purse in his pocket out of which he gives his grandchildren a pound when he sees them.

He writes books and sermons and speeches. His books are mainly on religious topics and his speeches are mainly on political issues.

He travels on aeroplanes at least once a month to go to Brussels or Strasbourg and once every week to go to London. A couple of times a year he travels further away to places like America, Africa or Singapore to preach.

When he is very tired he falls asleep in his large black reclining leather chair and sometimes he snores very loudly.

He is very well known everywhere he goes and has police protection all the time.

Every day he does something different so he is never fed up with doing the same thing day after day. The only day in the week that he has the same kind of routine is a Sunday when he preaches in his own church twice and somewhere different each Sunday afternoon.

He works long hours from early morning until late at night or even early on the next morning.

He enjoys his work and is always enthusiastic about it.

He is very loving and caring and I love him very much.

He is my Papa Paisley.

by Lydia Huddleston, written when she was 11 years old.
Lydia is the eldest of Dr. & Mrs. Paisley's
seven grandchildren.

SHARON HUDDLESTON

There is a lot to be said about time in the Bible. If we want to serve God we need *understanding of the times* (I Corinthians 12:32). We should *leave our times in God's hand.* (Psalm 31:15). We need to know that *the Lord is our strength in the time of trouble.* (Psalm 37:39) and that *He is also our salvation in the time of trouble.* (Isaiah 33:2). We are instructed to *redeem the time* (Ephesians 5:16).

In the book of Esther we read these words of Mordacai to his niece Queen Esther, *"and who knoweth whether thou art come to the kingdom for such a time as this?"* (Esther 4:14). Matthew Henry comments on this question by saying, "We should every one of us consider for what end God has put us in the place where we are, and, when any particular opportunity of serving God and our generation offers itself, we must take care that we do not let it slip."

For more than fifty years Dad has been doing just that, serving God and our generation in every circumstance and opportunity, whether religious or political, whether at home with the family or in the wider community of church or state. Dad is always the same man with the same stand, same message and same principles. No one can be in any doubt about what he believes and Whom he serves.

FOR SUCH A TIME AS THIS - RELIGIOUSLY

Dad's text is Ephesians 6:19 and 20 "And for me, that utterence may be given unto me, that I may open my mouth boldly, to make known the mystery of the gospel, for which I am an ambassador in bonds: that therein I may speak boldly as I ought to speak." This is a text that Dad has made his own. In 1951 Dad founded the Free Presbyterian Church of Ulster to stand up for Bible principles, teachings and morals which were being abandoned by many of the so-called main denominations. In doing so he caused anger among certain quarters of the established churches, many of those attending the first service of the Free Presbyterian Church in Crossgar were spat upon and verbally abused. This did not deter Dad but made him more determined to do the right. Being imprisoned twice for his persistent stand for his beliefs was a time of emptiness and loneliness for Dad and the rest of the family. Through all this Dad's faith increased in strength.

Dad's religion was not for the public only but also for the family. From my earliest days I can remember being told the stories from the Bible and how I needed to ask Jesus into my heart to wash away my sins. I also remember how, when I went out with Dad in the car, he would ask me what Bible story Mum had told me the previous night before going to bed. Sometimes I confused the names or the way God had done things. On one occasion, when recounting my version of Adam and Eve being driven out of the Garden of Eden. I told Dad that God put Adam and Eve in his car and drove them out of the garden. When Dad enquired if Mum had said what kind of car it was, I replied, "No, but I think it was a big Jag." I thought God must have a Jaguar as this was the biggest and most expensive car I knew at the age of three!

Of course, Dad was at home more when Rhonda and I were small as he was not yet in political life and so our early childhood holds precious memories for Rhonda and myself. Family worship was conducted every morning before we went to school, when Dad read the Bible and we all in turn, from the eldest to the youngest, prayed. When Dad was absent from home, whether preaching the gospel across the world or when he was in prison, Mum read and then we all prayed. One morning everything was running later than usual and so Mum read and decided we would pray in the car on the way to school. On the North Road we had a slight bump in traffic and when the man from the car in front came to see what had happened, he recognised Mum and said, "Mrs Paisley, what happened? Are you alright?" to which Mum replied, "We're fine, we were praying." This reply got a rather strange and surprised look from the man. Fortunately, no damage was done to either car! We often laugh about this incident.

FOR SUCH A TIME AS THIS - POLITICALLY

When Dad was called of God to go into politics it was a very serious time in our Province. Many people sneer and say ministers of the gospel should not be involved in politics, it's not a place for Christians. Perhaps they should read their Bibles where they would find out about men like Joseph and Daniel, to give but two examples, who took their stand in the affairs of their land. Who else in our day of 'political correctness' would stand up in the European Parliament in Strasbourg and call the Pope the Anti-Christ to his face? This was not an easy task for Dad, it took great courage, but Dad knew he had to do it. He was kicked and beaten in the Parliament by members who vehemently opposed what he did. We read in God's Word in the book of Samuel, "them that honour me I will honour" and in Matthew chapter 10, "Whosoever therefore shall confess me before men, him will I confess also before my Father which is in heaven". No one in the European Parliament, Westminster or the Northern Ireland Assembly has to ask what Dad believes and where he stands on any issue, it is plain to see what his stand is.

FOR SUCH A TIME AS THIS - INTERNATIONALLY

Dad has travelled around the world preaching the gospel and seeing many precious souls won for the Lord. He has been on missionary tours in Africa encouraging and upholding the missionaries there and to Peru and Romania to encourage those of like precious faith. Dad also evangelises by the writing of many books and by his messages on tape which are sent around the world. His messages can also be found on the Internet. These books and tapes are of great benefit to those who have no church or fellowship in their area, and to those who are confined in their homes or in hosptials and nursing homes.

1999 has been a difficult year for Dad. He had to spend some time in hospital but while there had the opportunity to witness and see a man converted to Christ. He also had the long election campaign for the European Parliament and in this he once again confounded his enemies by topping the pole for the fifth successive time. He never fails to return thanks publicly to God after each election victory by singing the Doxology.

Dad has been God's man in the Twentieth Century and now into the Twenty-first Century where he will, with God's help, continue to serve God with all his might.

> *"God grant me this: the strength to do*
> *Some needed service here,*
> *The wisdom to be brave and true,*
> *The gift of vision clear,*
> *That in each task that comes to me*
> *Some purpose I may plainly see.*
>
> *God teach me to believe that I*
> *Am stationed at a post,*
> *Although the humblest 'neath the sky,*
> *Where I am needed most;*
> *And that at last, if I do well*
> *My humblest service will tell.*
>
> *God grant me faith to stand on guard,*
> *Uncheered, unspoken, alone,*
> *And see behind each duty hard*
> *My service to the Throne,*
> *Whate'er my task, by this my creed,*
> *I am on earth to fill a need."*

Sharon Huddleston is the eldest of the five Paisley children.

RHONDA PAISLEY

Had I choked to death on my broccoli last week I wouldn't be sitting writing my bit for this my father's latest book. No, I'm not being fatalistic but I very nearly did choke when my father began reminding me of my commitment and its due date.

We were together in Strasbourg and after a long, in fact a very long day, our evening meal had just been served. As we waited we had been discussing 'time'. Dad was using me as a sounding board for some of his ideas regarding this book and I was enjoying bouncing as many thoughts as possible back at him, (I learnt this skill from my mother!) some of which we laughed at thoroughly but they weren't exactly what he was looking for.

Anyway, reminding me that I too had to get something written was his way of getting me back, and realising I had zilch accomplished he continued with his exhortation. "And," he said, looking over his glasses at me, "I don't want anything controversial." You don't need me to explain why I nearly choked. In Strasbourg of all places he says this to me! I'm sure both my father and the pope would be just a tad disappointed if a Paisley wasn't up to being controversial. I hasten to add that my intention is not to live my life in a controversial manner. However, neither is it my intention to avoid controversy. You may agree or disagree, like or dislike, smile or cringe at what I do, the choice is yours.

Anyway, how I ever got roped into this contribution is more than I know! At this very minute I'd hang the publisher and my father until their necks were very painful. And, I bet (not that I ever do) that every other contributor at some stage in preparing his or her contribution felt exactly the same!

And - there you have it - anything worthwhile causes a degree of difficulty. To write this I must forego something else, albeit something of lesser value.

All my life I have been a witness to my parents' foregoing. I have seen them give up many things in order to accomplish something of greater value. Do I admire them for this? Yes. Do I respect them for this? Yes. But, most of all, I love them for it. As I review, with the eyes of a daughter, what they together have achieved I am honoured to have been a witness and to learn what it really is to forego.

We all "give up" things in life. It is the nature of the beast. But very few of us really forego anything at all. We mistake foregoing for swapping - a simple exchange of one thing for another - like money for a coat and probably a coat we don't even need! But to forego something is actually to go without. It is giving up something we need in order that something which another needs is gained. What an exchange! I strive to be big enough to forego.

It is not necessary for me to list all the things I have seen my parents forego. That would be unseemly and embarrass them greatly - in fact I couldn't even list everything because I am sure I don't know everything! This principle of surrender has guaranteed that the ministry my parents have dedicated their lives to has been blest, more than they ever could have believed. I use the word 'ministry' in its widest possible sense, encompassing all of their work and all of us, their children. Because they have obeyed, we in turn are blest.

I am the only one of my parents' children who is unmarried, and although I have spent time living outside Northern Ireland and although I am not the eldest in the family this fact means I have lived with my parents the longest, dear help them! I often joke about how rebellious they are!

Yes, I do still live at home - it's nice to have the opportunity to clear this up as I've heard many things about where I live and even who I've lived with. My mother is in her sixties, my father in his seventies, I have just entered my forties and I continue to see my parents put their ministry first. At a time when I as their child would wish to see them relax a bit and take it easier - dare I say it, retire! they seem only to get busier and, in spite of it all, thrive on it! Half times I'm dragging up behind, knackered, and they are still enthused and energised! Between you and me, I wouldn't have it any other way!

I know this book is about my father and his work but anyone who really knows my father would know that he comes with mum. They are a package, bound together in their love for one another and in their love for the Lord Jesus Christ.

People say many things about my father's work and abilities. Some of it I agree with, some of it I disagree with. Some of it makes me want to cuss (not that I ever would!) and some of it makes me laugh. But I would say to you, no matter how badly expressed, my personal experience as one of his children has value because it is related first-hand.

I know a huge percentage of people who read about my father want some juicy piece of info on him. Goodness, my brothers, sisters and I get saliva all over us from people drooling to get some titbit! There are others who give us the titbits, but occasionally they are very tasty little morsels and not at all malicious.

One afternoon I was waiting to cross Great Victoria Street and before the lights changed a little lady at my elbow nudged me and said, "You're one of the Paisley's aren't you. You have your mother's eyes." I smiled at her, hoping she would go away but she insisted I give her a few minutes because she wanted to tell me something. We walked down the road and she led me into Wright's shoe shop. I wasn't half embarrassed! She said as she went through the door, "There's plenty of seats in here, we can sit and talk because I can't stand for long, I have a bad foot." I was mortified but the staff, I must say, were most courteous and they let us sit and talk. She began her saga, we were there for almost an hour!

"I live in Hamill Street and years ago these two girls who worked in the offices at the paint factory used to pass our door every day. They were two lovely lookin' girls and always joking and laughing. My husband always said, "Some day that dark-haired girl will have a boyfriend and we'll never see her again," and sure enough this big tall fellow started to come for her. They were a very handsome couple. After she finished work in there we never did see her again. Years later my husband, who's now dead (God bless him), was watching TV with me and I had the cat on my knee. All of a sudden he yells so loud the cat jumps off my knee and runs up the stairs and I says, "What is it?" and he says, "Look at those two on TV - yon's that wee girl with the brown eyes and black hair and the big fella who used to come for her." I looked closer at the TV and sure enough it was them - Ian Paisley and his wife. She had just been elected to the Corporation. Well, we started to laugh and I went up the stairs to bring the cat down, for that's where he'd run and he wasn't allowed up the stairs, and I dragged him out from under the bed and started coming down stairs again. Now look at the height of me (she really did only come up to my elbow) because I am so small I always wore big high heels and what with me still laughing, and my husband still laughing, and the cat in my arms, and our steep stairs, and my stilettos, didn't I go and fall down the stairs. Now, I didn't really hurt myself apart from my toe. As the days passed didn't my toe get worse until eventually I couldn't get my shoe on and my husband insisted I go to the hospital."

At this point she bent over and undid her flat lace-up shoe. Then she pointed to her foot and said, "Look at that! you see how I've no toe - well that was your father and mother's fault!"

Have you ever wished the ground would swallow you up? I could see the headline in the Belfast Telegraph, "Woman seeks compensation from Paisley for missing toe."

She continued, "My husband told me when I was in hospital I should send for Ian Paisley and show him what happened to my foot." Then she added, much to my great relief, "Of course he was only joking but I always said if ever I met your daddy or mummy or one of you children I would tell them my story."

This lady and I have kept in touch ever since and my life has been enriched by the lovely letters she continues to send me.

I confess I am more and more ruthless about our privacy but I will happily shout from the roof-tops that my father is a good man. He and mum have given us their children the very best foundation to build our lives upon, because they gave us the news of salvation and the freedom to be ourselves.

They have understood and cherished our individual talents and needs. They taught by example because they had been taught by example. They are dearer to me than life. They forego and do so without grudging, and I am a benefactor.

That, my friend, is Christianity!

Rhonda Paisley is the second daughter of Dr. & Mrs Paisley.

CHERITH CALDWELL

If Martin Luther had had his way this book would never have been written. By now you will know the verse used in the title of this book comes from the book of Esther - a book which this great hero of Protestantism didn't think should be included in the Bible as the word 'God' is not mentioned in it. If you are enjoying this book so far you will be thankful that his opinion was not adhered to. When you read my piece you may wish that it had been!

When we were growing up Mum and Dad often described us as two families. There were Sharon and Rhonda the first family and then the "three wee ones" - Cherith and the twins - Kyle and Ian.

I am the first of these "three wee ones" - a term I despised when I was growing up. "Me - a wee one! I was older than those two monsters by a year, a month and a day exactly!"

The age gap has narrowed considerably over the years. Often people cannot tell which of us girls is the eldest and I have to remind them!

I am the only Paisley sibling at whose birth my Dad was present. I was not born prematurely nor did I arrive unexpectedly, but Mum and Dad planned that I be born at home.

I am sure if I were analysed by a shrink, a suggestion which has been made to me on numerous occasions, they would say that this had a profound effect on my relationship with my father. Perhaps they are right. I know that when he was imprisoned in 1966, before the birth of my brothers, Mum said I pined for him and was even physically sick until his release. The second time he was imprisoned in 1969 I was just over three years old and remember vividly the huge gates at the Crumlin Road, the rattling keys, clanking gates and the long tables separating us from Dad. We weren't allowed to touch him. I hated that place. No doubt that experience has hardened my view that prisons punish the innocent, not the guilty.

There is an old black and white picture which was taken on Dad's release. Our faces in that photograph tell more than a thousand words.

It is impossible for me to think of Dad without thinking of Mum. They are the perfect match. A winning team. How my mother coped with five children, her church work, council work, assembly work and all the other tasks she was committed to I will never know. Add to this the fact that when her husband was not in prison he was fighting elections, flying to Parliament, and preaching around the globe. Yet in all that time I don't think any of us ever felt 'neglected' by either of our parents. They were always there for us. They must have been under considerable stress at times yet as children we never detected it.

I have one child and one job and often find that hard going. Multiply that by five and I would be a physical and mental wreck!

My parents are unique and they were driven because of their beliefs and their conscience. They were not in politics for their own ego or social ambitions, nor were they on some sort of crazed power trip. They were in it for people, for their country and for their faith.

In this age of the political sound-bite, the Armani suit and the coolest website, we have lost sight of the sacrifices they and other stalwarts made, and the abuse they took because of their political and religious beliefs.

With age and experience I have become cynical about politics. My father is certainly a dying breed. I would find it extremely difficult to count on one hand the number of politicians I respect, let alone vote for - and some of them are dead!

When you are a child you tend to think every family is like your own. I soon found out how wrong this assumption was. My family was very different from that of my peers. Most dads were home by six o'clock. Even on Christmas Morning we couldn't open our presents until Dad had come home from the Crumlin Road Prison where he preached at a morning service. (As you can imagine this fuelled my resentment toward the place). It felt like an eternity standing with our faces pressed to the porch window waiting for Dad's old Ford Zephyr to arrive in the driveway.

Kids visiting us loved the novelty of having police guards at the gate. I learned to greatly resent this infringement. It wasn't until I got married and left home that I realised how precious your own privacy is. My parents will no doubt have to live with this intrusion for the rest of their lives. I hate this country for that.

My father's unusual dual role as leader of a political party and Moderator of a church meant that we were also scrutinised as minister's children.

As any minister's child, in any congregation, in any denomination, will tell you it isn't an easy role, especially if you are a girl. Nothing is beyond commenting upon or criticising. Most of it was usually on trivial matters like dress, make-up, earrings, going to see a film - all of which are personal choices for individual consciences. Every Christian holds, in addition to his personal faith, many opinions which they feel to be consistent with it. And maybe they are. But as C. S. Lewis the great Christian apologist says, we are to "defend Christianity, not 'my religion'. "

My parents brought us up to question everything. They taught us right from wrong but treated us as individuals with the right to hold opinions of our own. There was no subject in our home which was not discussed. I can honestly say, to this day, I could talk to my parents about anything. We asked questions and were given answers, not excuses or platitudes. Both my parents respect diversity in us and in themselves. I believe it is the spark in their own relationship. They are very different people, whose relationship has not eclipsed their individuality. I covet that and strive to achieve it in my own marriage.

I remember when Andrew and I decided to get married, Dad suggested that as we wanted a very small wedding, we should opt for St. Stephen's Crypt in the House of Commons, Westminster, where MPs' families are permitted to get married. I flew over to London and met Mum and Dad for a day and we arranged everything in the space of a few hours. One thing about Dad - he gets things done. We went on a whistle-stop tour, taking in the Lord Chamberlain's Office, the Archbishop of Canterbury's Secretary, a London hotel and finally a visit to a florist. Bear in mind this was in July and our wedding was in August!

Of course, the rumours started. Why such a quick wedding? Some people's noses were twitching from the smell of the smoke from the shot gun. I heard every conceivable story - how sad my father was at my not getting married in the Martyrs Memorial, how I was marrying a Catholic from London and everyone was so disappointed in me. I honestly think some people were disappointed that none of this was true.

A Catholic from London? - whose mother spent many hours wrapping the Protestant Telegraph in the old Church Hall on the Ravenhill Road!

Thank God not everyone is so petty and narrow-minded. I count myself extremely fortunate to have found a partner and a family who saw beyond a surname and an image.

As a parent now myself, I treasure the times that Shane spends with his Nana and Papa Paisley and Granny Caldwell. I can already see the added dimension they give to his life and am grateful for it. I remember my own grandparents, especially Nana and Papa Cassells who were with us until I was in my teens. Of course, just like Shane, I didn't realise at the time the influence they were on me, but as I look to the new millennium I feel their presence still and know that Shane too will look back on these days with a sense of joy at ever having known those who were brought to the kingdom for such at time as this.

Cherith Caldwell is the youngest of the three Paisley daughters.

REV. KYLE PAISLEY

"For if thou altogether holdest thy peace at this time, then shall there enlargement and deliverence arise to the Jews from another place; but thou and thy father's house shall be destroyed: and who knoweth whether thou art come to the kingdom for such a time as this?" Esther 4:14. This text of Scripture sums up for me the value of Dad's influence in the political affairs of Ulster and more especially in family life and church life.

It gives all of us an immense amount of pleasure to see how God has used him where He has placed him in public life as well as in private.

Esther 4:14 relates to a most critical period for the captive Jews in Persia. They were threatened with genocide through Haman's manipulation of the political system. He slandered the Jews to the king, saying that they were rebels against his law and a threat to the state. So Ahasuerus was provoked into giving commandment for their destruction. Haman was an Agagite, a descendant of Agag the Amalekite. The Amalekites were idolaters and Israel's ancient enemy. So here is a case of religious bigotry seeking to overthrow an innocent people through political machinations. The Jews were naturally sorrowful. Esther grieved for her people too. But she was also better placed than anyone else to avert the genocide, for she was the king's wife and if any could win his heart over, she could. It is no wonder then that Mordecai, her uncle, said to her: "Who knoweth whether thou art come to the kingdom for such a time as this?"

As subsequent events show, Esther was the right person in the right place, at the right time.

She took the matter to heart and wept.

She took the matter to God and prayed.

She took the matter in hand and worked - even laying her own life on the line, not knowing when she went into the king if he would hold out the golden sceptre to her, signifying that she was spared and that she had his heart. This was her attitude "If I perish, I perish." Her one thought was the welfare of her people, which she secured and thus averted the threatened disaster. She was come to the kingdom at the right time.

I am reminded of Dad's political career. The situation in Ulster is very like the situation of the Jews in Esther's day. False religion (Romanism and ecumenism) along with political corruption, threatens civil freedom and religious freedom. The opportunity to preach the pure Gospel of Christ as revealed in the Bible, will certainly be diminished if the present aim of our enemies is realised, which is a united Ireland. Many innocent people have lost their lives in the push that has already been made in that direction. Many more will die if it comes about.

I believe (along with many others) that God raised up Dad for such a crisis. He certainly has taken the situation in Ulster to heart, and to God, and in hand, and no doubt the Lord has helped him in the position that he is in, to thwart the plans of those who intend to destroy Biblical Protestantism in Ireland. He has "come to the kingdom for such a time as this", and it is a privilege and pleasure to see him so used.

However dedicated Dad has been in seeking Ulster's welfare, he has not pursued this to the neglect of his children's welfare - particularly our spiritual welfare. I am thinking of something that happened to me when I was in my early teens. It was for me a particularly difficult time because of doubts regarding my salvation. Had I repented enough since trusting Christ as Saviour? Had I prayed enough? Had I read the Bible enough? These were a few of the questions which constantly bombarded my mind. It seemed that I could never get away from them. I brooded over them and came to the conclusion that I was not saved after all. As well as this, terrible thoughts about God filled my mind, thoughts that I never devised or cherished, but they came and I could not explain why. Eventually I concluded that I could never be saved. This increased my depression. This was the worst experience of my life thus far.

Only those who have been through such an experience understand what I mean. The situation in Esther's day was seemingly irrecoverable. I felt mine was too. Fortunately I was wrong, and I had the help I needed for "such a time". Though very busy with many other important matters, Dad on numerous occasions took time to deal with my problem. Sometimes at night I would be particularly troubled, not wanting to sleep in case, after all, my profession of faith was a false one and being unconverted I would wake up in Hell. Both Dad and Mum had a great deal of patience at that time, but it paid off. Dad pointed me to the Word of God, to that wonderful promise in John 6:37 "Him that cometh unto me I will in no wise cast out." This settled the matter for me, for having come to Christ and received Him as my Saviour I knew on the authority of His own Word that He had taken me in!

I don't know what I would have done if I had a father who was not a Christian and not able to give me Biblical advice! God had the right man in the right place at the right time! In this sense for me Esther 4:14 is applicable - he had "come to the kingdom for such a time as this".

The text is also applicable to the influence he has had in the formation and forward movement of the Free Presbyterian Church. He had to make sacrifices in order to help establish it. It was not welcomed by a lot of people, particularly at its inception and early years, and is still hated a great deal by many. So no one can say that the part he has played in it was motivated by a desire for popularity. He was popular before its formation, with large congregations attending the various Gospel missions that he conducted around the Province. The venture was undertaken simply out of a genuine love for the honour of Christ and the truth of the Bible which we are commanded to hold to and never sell (Proverbs 23:23).

The growth of the Free Presbyterian Church, the influence it has had in encouraging Christians to separate from the doctrinal apostasy of various religious bodies and from those who are seeking unity with the Roman Antichrist, its spread to many other parts of the world - for all these things we give the Lord the glory. Yet God has condescended to use human instruments to forward the witness of the Gospel in the world and it is only right that those who have been thus used should be recognised. The Bible commands that they are to be held in honour who have laboured in the Word (I Timothy 5:17). I have no doubt that the witness to Christ's name that has been made by the Free Presbyterian Church has been successful because of the leadership that Dad has given.

No doubt, if Esther had not seized the moment for her people then deliverance would have arisen from another place (Esther 4:4). The fact remains that she did seize the moment and thus God used her in a wonderful way, when she was prepared to lay her all on the line. I feel that Dad has done just this in his church life, and the example this leaves for the present and succeeding generations of Free Presbyterians is not to be underestimated. The ministers and members owe a debt of gratitude for his leadership and example. The way the church has been used to inform and encourage Christians to the kind of militancy that the Lord desires from those who profess His name, shows in another sense that he was on the scene and on the job at the right time, that he was "come to the kingdom for such a time as this".

I am personally thankful to God that He has given me such a father. All his children are proud of him.

Kyle Paisley is the twin son of Dr. and Mrs. Paisley and Minister of Oulton Broad Free Presbyterian Church, Lowestoft, England.

IAN PAISLEY JNR

When I was a wee lad growing up in Belfast I attended my father's church on the Ravenhill Road. Sundays were always long days, long in the sense that time seemed to slow down from the clockwork precision movement of school days and a fast past Saturday of play and fun. By contrast Sunday was slower. A time of contemplation in a regimented order of church, Sunday lunch, Sunday school, church and home to bed. However, sometimes after the evening service, we would go out with Mum and Dad to a friend's house. There my twin brother and I would eat supper and sometimes entertain the other guests and at times other close friends or visiting pastors or else, if they were uninterested, entertain ourselves until we became unruly, or time for home had arrived.

I didn't realise it then, but when I was a youngster I contemplated the meaning of time. It's not surprising now when I look back on it and think about my childhood. Our church has a massive clock on it with the inscription TIME IS SHORT. As a kid I had a fascination with clocks and watches. My mother recalled to me how when I was only about two or three she wondered why I was so quiet in the dining room. You can always be sure when a Paisley is quiet they are up to something or when they are smiling they are coming from or going to mischief! Back in the dining room I was busily engaged in pulling apart the delicate chiming mechanism of a much prized mantle clock. It must have been the little hammers and the chime bars that fascinated me, and an inquisitive mind that wanted to see how they worked. Unfortunately for the mantle clock, it was not indestructible. For many years this now hollowed-out clock remained a self-made toy that was never able to chime and certainly incapable of telling the time. A useless, dumb instrument. I'll return to some others in a moment!

As I said, clocks and watches fascinated me as did time itself. Dad had a friend - one of those kindly people we would visit after church - whose business was jewellery and watches. He was very kind and long-suffering to us terrible twins. On some Sundays, when we were obviously making too much noise and being a right pain, he would break the inevitable trail that would lead to us being told off by our parents, by taking us down into his safe room where he kept unmentionable numbers of jewels and watches and clocks.

It was truly an Aladdin's cave for two little boys. Our eyes must have stood out like organ stops because our friend took real pleasure in showing us some of the magnificent treasures he stored in this safe room. Sometimes, usually when it was close to our birthday or Christmas, he would let us select a grown up watch or a clock that we could take home and keep. It was fantastic. Not some half-baked, plastic junk watch but a real one which was so large it hardly fitted our juvenile wrists.

I remember choosing a beautiful one with a blue face and silver bezel which lasted me until I was a teenager when my arm had just about grown enough to fit the watch, but when the watch had given up the ability to work accurately. I still have it stored away in a box in the attic. Watches fascinated me for years after - they still do. The way they work, the way they look,. Yet, at the end of it all, no matter how fancy, no matter how expensive, they perform one simple task - they tell the time, usually associated with the 'here and now' time of what hour of the day it is, but the concept of time is encapsulated by them.

Sitting in church as a boy this idea of time must have played on my mind. In our hymnbook after most hymns is the name of the author and usually the dates they lived. I remember quite vividly, (in fact I still do it today), looking at those dates and consciously subtracting them one form another in order to figure out the length of time that hymn writer had on this earth. Sometimes it seemed such a long time, spanning two centuries such as 1743-1816 when in reality it was only a short 73 summers and winters of life come and gone. Other dates seem much shorter, representing a life lived out in the same century.

To a child time is long. It seems it will last forever. What's all the fuss about? But now looking back we realise how quickly it has really propelled past us. We stand on the verge of a new century, indeed a new millennium - I started life in 1966 and hope to finish some time in two thousand and something, but in all reality it has been short. Just a vapour, like dew on celestial grass that by daybreak has gone. I now know why my father placed that clock with the giant words on the front of our church and why as a boy I often heard him repeat the refrain "time is short, it will soon be past, and only what's done for Jesus will last."

For such a time as this, the new century needs people who know the value of time, not the value of timepieces; who know how to squeeze out of every day its full value in terms of work for those things that are really important.

I now have two daughters of my own. Like any parent I know what they make of time. "When will we be there?" "How many minutes will it take?" and with tears and sobs, "It takes too long Daddy," are cries I often hear and have to answer. But how swiftly our children spring up and how quickly they have come to represent the passing of time. From helpless new-born babies to troublesome toddlers to aspiring schoolgirls, they represent to their mother and me how rapidly time is passing, and how little time we have as parents and as Christians to see our loved ones won for Christ. I once heard my father preach a sermon where he used the phrase "redeeming the time". What a promise this holds for us all! Time lost in this century we can with diligence, prayer and work, redeem. A commodity so happily given to us and so carelessly we thought we had lost, has now become a valued asset we can use for tomorrow.

In our family I am the "name sake", the son who bears his father's name - his father's "great" name. But, as I sometimes remind him It's not his name but mine! Some time ago he gave me it and I hope I have some time left to both live up to it and use it for my own. All we have in time is our name. When someone has passed theirs on to you it becomes a remarkable privilege to possess. In effect, whether he wanted to or not, he has entrusted me with the only thing he has - his name.

People still say to me "what's it like being called after your father?" or "what's is like having Ian Paisley as your dad?" It's something that has never cost me a second thought. My name I have never considered to be anyone else's, even someone as close as my Dad. As time has moved on, of course, I have realised the fuller meaning of this simplistic request for information from many simpletons who did not realise just how foolish their question really was.

My father has been a tremendous influence on my life. Through his preaching I came to understand that in time I must make a decision that will last all eternity, a decision I learnt from him but made in the arms of a caring mother. And through his politics I have come to learn that we are only responsible for the time that we are in politics; that we have been given a duty and a privilege to advocate our cause, not as something we possess but as something we borrow from our children's children.

In time I have found out how important it is to be honest and true to my beliefs no matter what the cost, the insult or the ridicule. And I have seen my father hated, despised, treated like dirt by people who, frankly, are not fit for him to place his heel upon, the so-called great, wise and good who have grown fat and pompous in time and will, tragically, burn in eternity, except they receive Christ.

My father should not have survived this long in time, given the odds he has waged against, but he whose worthy name I bear has proved to be the rock against which others break themselves. Long may that be the case in such a time as this!

Ian Paisley Jr is the twin son of Dr and Mrs Paisley